Learning to Teach

Primer on Teacher Education Methods

Learning to Teach

Primer on Teacher Education Methods

by

Sue L. T. McGregor
McGregor Consulting Group

INFORMATION AGE PUBLISHING, INC.
Charlotte, NC • www.infoagepub.com

Library of Congress Cataloging-in-Publication Data

CIP record for this book is available from the Library of Congress
http://www.loc.gov

ISBNs: 979-8-88730-410-6 (Paperback)

979-8-88730-411-3 (Hardcover)

979-8-88730-412-0 (ebook)

Printed in the United States of America

CONTENTS

PREFACE

This primer is about learning how to teach. As its name suggests, it provides a *basic* introduction to what is involved in becoming an effective, efficient, and efficacious educator. Respectively, this means doing the right things, doing things right, and getting things done while feeling one has made a difference (Le Cunff, 2021). The targeted audiences are (a) preservice teachers (PST) (i.e., nonprofessional student teachers enrolled in a college or university Bachelor of Education degree or diploma), (b) early-career (novice) in-service teachers or (c) any educator for that matter who wants to build or bolster their essential foundation for teaching.

The content deals with what is commonly called, *teacher education methods*. Related courses are usually taught in college or university *education* programs (e.g., Bachelor of Education [BEd] degree). Method is Latin *methodos*, "pursuit of knowledge" (Harper, 2022). As the name implies, PSTs take *methods* courses to help them *pursue* (attain) knowledge about how to teach. The term *teacher education methods* refers to the principles, philosophies, theories, and on-the-ground strategies that teachers judiciously use to ensure students' learning. Batchelor (2012) warned that breadth of coverage in these methods' courses can take precedence over depth (i.e., comprehensiveness, thoroughness). When this happens, early-career teachers may not be equipped with the necessary competencies when entering the labor market.

Appreciating this real possibility, this primer, with its focus on the basics, breaks down the many facets of teaching to ensure richer understandings of the nitty gritty of being an educator. The primer is unabashedly oriented to a synthesis of the technical (how-to) aspects of teaching (grounded in philosophy and theory) because without prowess in these skills, even the most dedicated teacher may not be effective and efficient let alone

Learning to Teach: Primer on Teacher Education Methods, pp. ix–x
Copyright © 2024 by Information Age Publishing
www.infoagepub.com

efficacious. This primer does not focus on the sociocultural/political aspects of teaching, teaching as inquiry, or how to develop thinking educators, as these important topics are addressed elsewhere.

Furthermore, teaching is both an art and a science. "There is artistry in the way teachers connect with students and foster their understanding. At the same time, there is a science to teaching and learning, an evidence base on which to build our approaches to developing students' knowledge, skills, and competencies" (Bouffard, 2018, para. 1). This primer is about the science of teaching with a significant nod to educational philosophies and curriculum theories.

Most educators function within a learning-delivery system comprising five curricular components, which can take years to finish. (a) The complete program of study (the *official curriculum*) unfolds over years or months (often including *several courses*). (b) Individual *courses* last on average three months or longer (called semesters or terms) unless condensed for some reason (e.g., summer school). (c) Each course is broken down into smaller, self-contained, but sequentially related, *modules* (lasting months or weeks), which in turn comprise (d) even smaller *units* that last weeks or days. (e) The *units* are further broken down into daily, individual *lesson plans* lasting on average 30–90 minutes, longer if a laboratory experience (Fleck, 1980; Posner & Rudnitsky, 2001).

To accommodate this system, this primer adopts a *before-during-after* class approach. It addresses how to (a) prepare lessons *before* a class (learning styles, learning objectives, lesson planning, and learning environments); (b) deliver lessons *during* a class (instructional strategies, questioning strategies, and classroom management); and (c) evaluate learning *after* the class (student assessment and evaluation strategies, and teacher self-reflection).

This basic tool kit is further underscored with details about the larger constructs of developing courses, modules, and units from which daily lessons emerge. Higher level notions of educational philosophies, curriculum theories, curriculum development approaches, and kinds of curriculum are also included to illustrate how they, as the educational context, shape teachers' pedagogies—their ideas about who, what, why, how, where, and when to teach.

As a caveat, the approach herein is most appropriate for public and private school teachers who deal with *pedagogy* (children, youth, and adolescent learning). University instructors may benefit as well, but they engage with *andragogy* (adult learning), which involves different assumptions, principles, theories, and strategies of learning and teaching than those used to teach children, youth, and adolescents (Knowles et al., 2011).

CHAPTER 1

EDUCATIONAL CONTEXT
Philosophical and Theoretical

This chapter provides a brief but comprehensive overview of higher order constructs informing PST education and teaching practice. The spirit of these constructs is shared herein anticipating that those interested will read further. This chapter *primes* PSTs and novice teachers to appreciate the significant impact that educational philosophies, curriculum theories, and curriculum development approaches have on their teaching—often without being consciously aware of it. But everyone has "a philosophy of education; it's there just under the surface; unseen but affecting every decision you will make as a teacher" (Petronicolos, 2011, p. 1).

EDUCATIONAL PHILOSOPHIES

A philosophy is a belief system that guides behavior. It is an internal system that each person builds to help guide conduct in their life (Harper, 2022)—their philosophy of life. An *educational* philosophy thus guides behavior relative to education whether a teacher, administrator, curriculum developer, policymaker, policy pundits, researcher, parent, or guardian, even student. An educational philosophy reflects a person's assumptions about and shapes their perceptions of (a) the purpose of education and a particular educational program; (b) what content is of value and worth learning; (c) how students learn; (d) what materials, methods, instructional strategies, and resources to use to teach them; and (e) how, when, and by whom learning should be assessed and evaluated (McGregor, 2019; Ornstein, 1991; Sowell, 2000).

Learning to Teach: Primer on Teacher Education Methods, pp. 1–17
Copyright © 2024 by Information Age Publishing
www.infoagepub.com

Several key educational philosophies can inform curricular design and teaching pedagogy: perennialism, essentialism, academic rationalism, curriculum as technology, cognitive learning, self-actualization (personal relevance, humanistic), progressivism, social reconstructivism, personal-global, and existentialism (Oliva, 2001; Parkay & Hass, 2000; Sowell, 2000). In this primer, these philosophies are categorized as teacher-centered, student-centered, and macro-centered learning (see extensive details in Table 1.1, which should be read in its entirety).

Teacher-Centered

As an overview, *teacher-centered learning* focuses on content and subject matter (e.g., information, facts, competencies) and depends on the teacher acting in the expert role with students as passive vessels waiting to be filled up. They are rote learners who memorize and master predetermined content. If students do not learn, they have failed rather than the teacher failing to teach effectively (Collins & O'Brien, 2003).

Student-Centered

In contrast, *student-centered learning* views students as self-directed, self-motivated, and self-regulated learners who can take control of their educational experiences while depending on the teacher as a coach, guide, and facilitator or some combination. Teachers structure the learning environment so that students can influence the learning process and learn independently, alone, and with others (Collins & O'Brien, 2003).

Macro-Centered

The neologism *macro-centered learning* was coined herein to capture educational philosophies that are concerned with life beyond teachers and students: society, nature, and humanity. Macro is Greek *makros*, "large scale, long period of time" (Harper, 2022). Students are encouraged to learn that they are connected to life larger than themselves, and that their actions have broad consequences for a long time. The latter eventuality requires education to prepare students to be responsible, holistic, and integrated thinkers—lifelong learners. Lifelong learning pertains to the voluntary, self-motivated, and sustained pursuit of knowledge to augment personal and professional growth and advancement (Ireland Department of Education and Science, 2000).

Table 1.1

Common Educational Philosophies

Teacher-Centered Learning	
Perennialism	• per its name (lasting for a long time), perennialism assumes the truth is the same today as it was in the past; look to the past to solve today's problems. • instead of truth as facts, truth comprises everlasting, unchanging *principles* and enduring *great ideas* that serve all humankind. • teach *universal truths* through Liberal Arts curricula using both (a) "the Classics" (e.g., Dickens, Steinbach, Joyce, Hemingway, Shakespeare, Austen, Brontë) and (b) other *enduring* disciplines (e.g., mathematics, science, engineering). • lead by the teacher, students learn universal *truths* through reasoning, logic, rational thinking, revelation, the scientific method, and the Socratic method (i.e., cooperative, argumentative dialogue).
Essentialism (basic skills, 3Rs, liberal education)	• like its namesake, teach what is *essential* to transmit national and cultural heritage—*preserve society* the way it is as much as possible appreciating that change may have to happen. • focus on *essential* skills and the *intellectual and moral standards* needed for students to cope with and adjust to existing society; called a *common core* of knowledge. • students learn the essentials, rigorously and thoroughly, from simple to complex, by studying traditional basic subjects: 3Rs (reading, writing, and arithmetic), science, classical art, history, literature. • teach *facts* not principles using content preselected by curriculum experts and teachers; students have no say—they have to *master* the essentials to preserve society (and pass the course). • core curriculum may have to change so students can still be taught to value hard work, respect authority, learn self-discipline, and accept societal standards rather than challenge them.
Academic Rationalism (disciplinary mastery)	• per its name, this approach deifies (privileges) *reason*. • intent is to prepare citizens who can make *rational* judgements and partake in an existing society by dealing with duty, truth, being, and beauty. • using subject matter deemed *worthy* of study (e.g., science, mathematics, and literature), curricula cultivate students' intellect so they can reason; precludes so-called fringe subjects, which are erroneously presumed to dilute ability to learn how to reason (e.g., family studies, music, drama, arts, physical education, industrial arts). • assumes that, unless *all* schools teach only a core of worthy subjects that students must *master*, a common educational foundation will be missing in society, which will then suffer due to lack of logical and well-reasoned citizenry action.

(Table continued on next page)

Table 1.1 (Continued)

Common Educational Philosophies

Teacher-Centered Learning	
Curriculum as Technology (outcome based)	• now called *outcome-based* education (OBE), this approach depends on students *mastering* education-authority mandated and teacher-selected content. • sequenced organization of content is presumed to ensure *efficient* learning (i.e., productive learning with no wasted effort). • also called the *teach-to-the-test* approach, it depends on *standardized* testing and routinized and *rote learning* (memorization). • teachers and state (education policy makers) create *mensurable* behavioral objectives (intended learning outcomes [ILOs] and learning objectives). • this task-focused learning has a heavy focus on *competencies* and predetermined *standards* and often uses technology to deliver the curriculum (e.g., computer assisted learning [CAL]).
Cognitive Learning Processes	• *cognition* means the mental acquisition of knowledge and understandings through thinking, experience, and senses. • cognitive learning thus assumes that, because it is impossible to know everything, teachers must show students *how to think*. • students thus learn *how to inquire* and *investigate* instead of learning just content (just facts, information, or enduring principles). • subject matter is a tool to develop *intellectual prowess*; students gain thinking skills they can use well into their lives far beyond the formal classroom. • the curriculum is *process oriented* rather than task oriented. • students learn how to think in all sorts of circumstances by problem posing and problem solving—*thinking* their way through life (i.e., lifelong learners and thinkers).
Student-Centered Learning	
Self-actualization (personal relevance, humanistic, holistic)	• focus is on helping learners realize their full potential and aid in their individual development, growth, and autonomy (self-regulation, self-direction, self-determination). • because the intent is for students to learn how to cope with problems that have personal significance, teachers choose topics and content matter that are relevant and meaningful to students (authentic to them). • teacher is facilitator who balances students' interests with social-cultural needs. • rather than teaching students how to solve social issues, these issues and curricular content are *used* to help students become self-evolved, self-governing *agents*. • teacher provides a resource-rich learning environment so students can explore and "come into themselves."

(Table continued on next page)

Table 1.1 (Continued)

Common Educational Philosophies

Student-Centered Learning	
Progressivism	• very child-centered approach; considered forward thinking because it challenges the traditional perennial, essentialism, and academic rationalism approaches where students have no voice or say in what they learn, how, or when. • intent is to create *independent thinkers* acting for the *public good*, meaning classrooms are *democratic* and include *moral* education and *character building* to foster self-esteem and self-worth. • curriculum intentionally meets the needs of each child who develop at different rates. • content (chosen by teacher *and* students) reflects children's experiences, interests, and abilities; teachers are "in charge," but students do as much as they can; students are viewed as *learning partners*. • students *learn by doing* with others (i.e., experiment, explore, discover).
Macro-Centered Learning	
Social Reconstructivism	• learning is for the *betterment of society*; shared societal values are central and take precedence over individuals' needs. • schools serve society, so the needs of society and social issues determine curricular content; the latter reflect pressing problems facing *humankind*. • intent is to reform (*reconstruct*) society through schools; therefore, schools must teach students how to be *socially responsible*, *critically conscious*, and *active participants* in social change. • students learn critical thinking, how to deal with controversial issues, self-reflection, and gain self-awareness.
Personal-global (transformative)	• this is a blend of the cognitive, self-actualization, and social reconstructivism philosophies—leading to *transformation* and change (also called global education and more recently education for sustainable development [ESD]). • through a *future-oriented* curriculum, students are taught to live and responsibly participate in a globally interdependent society. • the *well-being* of the entire world (humanity, other species, ecosystems, and the planet) is the focus of curricula ensured through teaching sustainability, personal responsibility, holistic and integrated thinking, global citizenship, ecological stewardship, interdisciplinary thinking, vanguard transdisciplinary thinking, critical and creative thinking, and self-reflection. • each person is continually in the process of *becoming* while seeking full personal *integration* into changing environments to ensure *social change*.

(Table continued on next page)

Table 1.1 (Continued)

Common Educational Philosophies

Macro-Centered Learning	
Existentialism	• Latin *existentia*, come into being; existentialism means a focus on *humanity* as a whole, the *human condition*, and the human *existence*; curricula help students learn about *being* and how they came to *be*
	• students are taught to analyze the human condition (e.g., poverty, war, freedom, justice, sustainability, equality, oppression, exploitation, free will)
	• to cope and deal with what they learn, students are also taught that they have the *freedom* to make choices, *but* those choices come with heavy *responsibilities* because every action has *consequences* for them and humanity.
	• hand in hand, students are taught to *question everything* (i.e., resist imposed answers and perspectives), which requires creating a space for students to both think *independently* and safely, *freely*, discuss heavy subjects and issues (serious, emotional, controversial, sensitive).
	• with teachers ensuring a strong focus and reliance on the arts, ethics, philosophy, drama, novels, music, theatre, and poetry, students grapple with the *meaning of life* (joy, angst, anger, suffering, hope, desires) as they strive to understand their *existence* as a human being.

CURRICULUM THEORIES

Not only do educational philosophies shape curricula but so do theories about how curricula are developed, structured, their content, and such. Theories are a system of ideas intended to explain something—a phenomenon, which is Greek *phainomenon*, "anything appearing that can be seen, viewed, observed" (Harper, 2022). Any theory's system is made up of three main ideas: (a) *assumptions* about a phenomenon; (b) *concepts and constructs* and their theoretical *definitions*; and (c) *propositions* about how the concepts and constructs relate to each other vis-à-vis explaining the phenomenon (McGregor, 2018). The specific theory of *curriculum* that curriculum planners, developers, and researchers use (knowingly or not) will profoundly shape the resultant curriculum or people's judgements of it (McGregor, 2018).

PSTs, indeed all teachers, must be aware of the powerful and subliminal (behind-the-scene) role that curriculum theories play, so they can understand their personal reactions to curricula developed, analyzed, and/or evaluated using particular theories. This theoretical appreciation may help PSTs understand their resonance with or push back against any given curriculum (McGregor, 2020). In this primer, curriculum theories were categorized into four types: structure, content, value, and process-oriented theories (per Glatthorn et al., 2011; Smith, 2000) (see Figure 1.1).

Figure 1.1

Four Types of Curriculum Theories

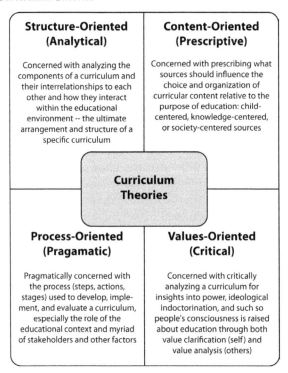

Structure-Oriented (Analytical)	Content-Oriented (Prescriptive)
Concerned with analyzing the components of a curriculum and their interrelationships to each other and how they interact within the educational environment -- the ultimate arrangement and structure of a specific curriculum	Concerned with prescribing what sources should influence the choice and organization of curricular content relative to the purpose of education: child-centered, knowledge-centered, or society-centered sources

Curriculum Theories

Process-Oriented (Pragamatic)	Values-Oriented (Critical)
Pragmatically concerned with the process (steps, actions, stages) used to develop, implement, and evaluate a curriculum, especially the role of the educational context and myriad of stakeholders and other factors	Concerned with critically analyzing a curriculum for insights into power, ideological indoctorination, and such so people's consciousness is raised about education through both value clarification (self) and value analysis (others)

Structure-Oriented Curriculum Theories

Structure-oriented theories are analytical in nature, meaning they examine in detail the elements of a *structure*, hence are so named. These theories concern the arrangement of and relations among the components of the structure of a complex curriculum and how these parts interact within the educational environment. Structure-oriented theorists want to know how these parts are (a) defined, (b) organized (by whom with varying degrees of power and influence) and (c) different from but connected with each other. Knowledge gained using these theories is useful to curriculum developers, evaluators, and researchers (Glatthorn et al., 2011).

Curriculum theorists using the structure-oriented approach might be concerned with (a) defining terms (e.g., curriculum, pedagogy, rationale, philosophy); (b) distinguishing how each term is related to but different from other terms (e.g., field of study versus program of study); (c) investigating how various curricular components interact with each other and within an educational context; (d) exploring how decisions about developing curricula are made at different levels (e.g., government, school board, university, think tanks); and (e) identifying principles that govern the selection and sequencing of content within, between, and among grade levels (Glatthorn et al., 2011). In short, what is involved in a curriculum coming into existence and the form or shape of its ultimate *structure*?

Content-Oriented Curriculum Theories

Content-oriented curriculum theories concern what content *should* be in a curriculum and what key sources should influence that content relative to the purpose of education. These theories intentionally specify the major sources that should influence the choice and organization of curricular *content*. They recommend and authorize certain sources over others, namely child-centered, knowledge-centered, or society-centered sources of curricular content (Glatthorn et al., 2011).

Child-Centered

These curriculum theories assume that the purpose of education is to ensure the child's emotional, social, physical, and cognitive development. Thus, what the child *needs* to know to become an autonomous, healthy, mature, empathetic, and responsible individual is what *should* be included in the curriculum rather than any specific subject matter or foci such as cultural heritage, society, or humanity (see Table 1.1) (Glatthorn et al., 2011).

Knowledge-Centered

These curriculum theories assume that disciplinary and subject matter content play a central role in building a curriculum and should be the major source of content. The curriculum content thus reflects what various disciplines deem important to know (e.g., science, mathematics, physical education, music, family studies). Other knowledge-centered theorists assume instead that these theories should focus on *how* children come to know things (i.e., multiple ways of knowing) (Glatthorn et al., 2011). A well-known example is Gardner's (2008) theory of multiple intelligences (see Chapter 3).

Society-Centered

These curriculum theories assume that the starting point of and prime influence on building a curriculum should be the social order, which is defined as an arranged system of social structures and institutions that brings stability to society (Cole, 2019). These theories assume that the purpose of curricula is to prepare citizens who can (a) conform to, (b) reform, (c) transform (with the future in mind) or (d) radically change (expose and repower) the existing social order. Courses should be developed that shape students along these specific trajectories with curriculum planners deciding on the preferred social order and educating students accordingly (Glatthorn et al., 2011).

Values-Oriented Curriculum Theories

This third theoretical orientation assumes that critically clarified and analyzed values should be the major source of content for a curriculum. Values-oriented theorists *critically* analyze and delve into whether an existing curriculum (a) perpetuates power differentials; (b) prevents or enables learners to be liberated; (c) indoctrinates students to predetermined societal roles and ideologies; or (d) reflects the curriculum designers' positionality (i.e., unquestioned biases, assumptions, and premises about legitimate knowledge). In effect, a values-oriented curriculum theory concerns unearthing how curricula can hinder or support raising people's consciousness by getting them to clarify their own values and analyze others' values so any ideological blinders and biases can be exposed and challenged. Knowledge thus gained should be used to reconceptualize education (Glatthorn et al., 2011).

Process-Oriented Curriculum Theories

Finally, process-oriented curriculum theories are pragmatic and focus on either (a) the actual process used to develop a curriculum (i.e., series of steps, actions, and stages) or (b) the process that *should* be used to develop a curriculum. Systematizing the process involved in coming up with new or revised curricula yields an organized system often reflected in flow charts—other people can follow the same process. This practical, application-focused approach is achieved by exploring the sequential and cyclical interplay among many elements and how they influence curriculum development alone or in some combination. These elements include but are not limited to actors, contextual factors, power and politics, deliberations and relational dynamics, organizational cultures (ethos) and structures, and problem-solving/conflict-resolution procedures. These elements can affect the efficiency and effectiveness of the formulation, implementation, and evaluation of the final end product whether formal curricula, courses, modules, units, or resources (Glatthorn et al., 2011).

CURRICULUM DEVELOPMENT APPROACHES

PSTs and novice teachers should also be familiar with how curricula are developed. Two basic approaches can be used: (a) implementation, technical (top down) and (b) enactment, nontechnical (bottom up) (Cho, 1998; Sowell, 2000). A top-down approach involves one person or an overarching committee dictating and controlling the process with nominal input or control from those at the bottom of the hierarchy who will be implementing it. Tasks are delegated and carried out down the chain with responsibility on completing the overall task falling to those at the top. Those at the bottom are usually expected to implement the imposed strategy or process despite having little say in its formulation. In contrast, the bottom-up approach to curriculum development respects the assumption that "two heads are better than one." It values drawing on many people to develop something. This collaborative approach gives everyone a say and bolsters the chances of overall acceptance of and benefit from the final outcome (Cho, 1998; Malsam, 2019; Sowell, 2000).

Top-Down Technical Implementation

The top-down "technical approach is so named because it assumes a rationale and systematic approach to designing an outcome-based, teacher-centered, objective, context-neutral curriculum created by nonteacher-populated committees" (McGregor, 2020, p. 34). A higher education authority representative hands down (imposes) the curriculum to teachers to implement despite their having little say in its development. There is an off chance of being invited as a content-expert specialist or for pilot testing before its official launch (McGregor, 2020). While some teachers welcome top-down curricula, others resist their imposition but have limited opportunity to push back against a legally mandated policy initiative—they must teach it. The top-down approach is mainly informed by the academic rationalism, essentialism, perennialism, and cognitive process educational philosophies (Sowell, 2000) (see Table 1.1).

The typical organizational format used to communicate a top-down curriculum's intent and contents comprises some combination of title, rationale, philosophy, goals, objectives, intended learning outcomes (ILOs), required topics and content, scope and sequence, instructional strategies, materials and resources, and assessment and evaluation of students' learning in addition to resource-focused appendices (Sowell, 2000). Although the rationale and philosophy elements provide insights into assumptions and theories shaping the curriculum (McGregor, 2020), teachers are most frequently drawn to the measurable learning outcomes and the scope and sequence sections (see next for details).

Measurable Learning Outcomes

Measurable learning outcomes are an inherent part of outcome-based education (OBE). Learning is Old English *leornung*, "study, action of acquiring knowledge," and outcome is a Middle English word meaning an emergence—that which results from something (Harper, 2022). An outcome is a situation that exists when something comes to an end. An outcome is also a consequence of doing something (Anderson, 2014). OBE is thus concerned with what arises or not from being exposed to learning something. Rao (2020) explained that "learning is supposed to have occurred when we can do something that we were not able to do earlier. [That *something* can include] acquiring new knowledge, behaviours, skills, values, preferences or understandings" (p. 6).

OBE is concerned with what students leave with not what they came in with. In addition to gauging what students have learned, results-obsessed OBE is used to judge the quality of the program within which students allegedly learn (Spady, 1994). Much ado is thus paid to how to write *good* measurable learning outcomes, which "are also referred to as Intended Learning Outcomes, Instructional Objectives, Educational Objectives, Behavioural Objectives, Performance Objectives, ... and Specific Learning Outcomes and Competencies" (Rao, 2020, p. 6) (see Chapter 3, this volume).

Scope and Sequence

This concept pertains to what to teach, in what order, at what depth, using what resources (North Dakota Department of Public Instruction [NDDPI], 2000). Scope (breadth and range of topics) and sequence (order and depth of coverage) also involve (a) *continuity* (dealing with content via multiple, progressive experiences within and across grade levels); and (b) *integration* (articulating how various topics, issues, and content are interrelated) (Sowell, 2000).

Scope and sequence documents are graphic representations of the major (a) curriculum elements, (b) standards of learning quality or (c) standards of learning attainment across grade levels. Usually presented in a matrix with rows, columns, and cells, the left column is the standard or element to be learned with the grade levels across the top (see Table 1.2). Each row across contains anticipated levels of learning for each standard with a *generic* description of the standard in respective cells in the far-left column (down). The expected level of learning *per* grade level is represented with benchmarks in each cell (i.e., points of reference for educators to use to discern expected level of learning) (NDDPI, 2000). Possible major elements for a Health Curriculum might be 1. Nutrition, 2. Growth and Development, 3. Mental Health, 4. Personal Health, and 5. Safety. An example of benchmarks (level of student achievement) is *Introduce* (I), *Reinforce* (R), *Master* (M), and *Escalate* (E) (see Table 1.2).

Table 1.2

Curriculum Scope and Sequence Chart Example

Major Curriculum Elements With Generic Descriptions	Standards (Benchmarks) of Anticipated Learning Quality and Attainment Per Grade Level					
	Grade 7	8	9	10	11	12
Element 1	I	R	R	–	–	–
2	I	R	R	M	–	v
3	–	–	–	I	R	M
4	–	I	R	R	M	E
5	–	–	I	R	M	E

Quite often, narrative is also inserted into individual cells to explain how learning is deepening or broadening from one grade level to another. To illustrate, in Table 1.2, the narrative for Grades 8 and 9 would be different for Element 1 with learning growing more detailed and complex. The scope and sequence process should ensure that no grade is overloaded with minimum redundancy among grades. There should be sufficient time (spread over grade levels) for major elements to be reinforced (R) before mastery (M) is expected, but mastery has to be achieved without excessive repetition from one grade to another (NDDPI, 2000). Reading a scope and sequence chart helps PSTs and novice teachers determine the scope of what is to be learned (range of topics) (far left column), their sequence across grade levels (rows), and the depth expected per grade level (row cells).

To illustrate, Element 5 is not introduced until Grade 9. Students are expected to be at an escalated level of expertise by Grade 12. Conversely, Element 1 is introduced in Grade 7, but students are never expected to master it, just get better at it. Each grade in Table 1.2 has on average three major elements some with a mix of introduction and reinforce (strengthen learning) and others with a mix of reinforce and master (solidify learning). Only higher grade levels are expected to reach an escalated (very intense and serious learning) level of learning and only for two of the five elements. Discerning this information from a scope and sequence chart helps PSTs figure out what to teach, in what order, at what depth, using what resources. They can further bolster their teaching by consulting with lower- and higher-grade teachers to see what they are doing (NDDPI, 2000).

Bottom-Up, Nontechnical Enactment

Much rarer in practice is the bottom-up, nontechnical, enactment approach to developing a curriculum. Enact means to create and make while doing something (Harper, 2022). Instead of using a preconceived, prescribed, and imposed top-down curriculum, the enacted curriculum "comes into being" (Sowell, 2000, p. 15) from the bottom up as it is collaboratively developed by students and teachers in a given context (Cho, 1998) (i.e., it is created while in progress). This enactment prompts student engagement in an atmosphere of shared power. As the curriculum is enacted (i.e., coauthored), students learn collaboratively and respectfully. The authoring process (i.e., creating, founding, and originating) yields an organic, living curriculum rather than an inorganic (not arising from natural growth), prescribed, and static curriculum (Sowell, 2000).

Instead of an arms-length, third-party committee, individual teachers are the main authors and architects of an enacted curriculum created while working in their community of learners. Teachers are "the major source of curriculum knowledge because they know their students and teaching contexts. They also know when the curriculum needs revision" (Sowell, 2000, p. 9). They *coauthor* the curriculum with students by respecting an authoring cycle that helps them plan the curriculum (Sowell, 2000). Not all learning outcomes are predetermined; many *emerge* as the curriculum is enacted with teachers drawing from seven knowledge bases (Shulman, 1987) to develop a curriculum for *their* context (see Table 1.3 used with permission from McGregor, 2020).

The enactment approach reflects the tenets of progressive (child-centered), holistic, global, and social reconstructivist educational philosophies (see Table 1.1), wherein learners and teachers, to varying degrees, cocreate *meaningful* learning experiences and results (outcomes) (Sowell, 2000). Learning is meaningful for students if it is relevant (i.e., connected to the matter at hand) and stays with them for life. What is learned can be applied in different contexts over time—it is enduring and still *means* something to them beyond the classroom (Oxford Learning, 2017).

Table 1.3

Seven Knowledge Bases for Teaching

- *content knowledge* (unique to disciplines and subdisciplines).
- *curricular knowledge* (state-approved plus other curricula, programs, materials, and resources related to content to be taught; also, curriculum development theory and approaches/models).
- *philosophical knowledge* (educational philosophies that determine beliefs about the aims of education shaped by the perceived relationship among education, learning, and society—transcends subject matter).
- *general pedagogical knowledge* (broad principles of classroom management, learning environment organization and communication, instructional strategies, assessment and evaluation, and personal pedagogical knowledge gained from experience and fuelled by beliefs and reflection—transcends subject matter).
- *knowledge of individual learners* themselves combined with *learning style theory*,
- *knowledge of educational contexts* (state and schoolboard governance and financing, community and cultural characteristics, laws and educational policies, educational research),
- *pedagogical content knowledge* (each teacher's personal and professional understanding of and expertise in melding subject matter content with how to teach informed by the previous six knowledge bases),

Table 1.4 contains a summary and comparison of the curriculum development approaches commonly called implementation and enactment. Marked differences exist along several common elements. Realistically, most PSTs and novice teachers will be teaching the top-down curriculum. That said, it is important that they know there is an alternative bottom-up approach that might better resonate with their own philosophy of education. Learners will benefit from their teachers' self-reflection on how approaches to curriculum development inform teaching vision and opinions about the purpose of education. A self-assured, philosophically aware teacher bodes well for student learning, and knowledge of the two main curriculum approaches enriches teachers' awareness (McGregor, 2020).

Kinds of Curriculum

Although this primer mainly concerns the top-down, implemented, official curriculum, PSTs should appreciate there are many kinds of curriculum (see Table 1.5 used with permission McGregor, 2022). That said, the formal, official curriculum they will be expected to teach is approved, printed, and distributed by a government's Department of Education or equivalent policy body. It includes curriculum guides, framework documents, outcome, and standard documents, and approved or state-authored textbooks and resources (Di Mascio, 2013). Its rationale and content are informed by a combination of disciplinary standards, best practice, prevailing ideologies, and convincing rhetoric (Whitson, 2005; Wilson, 2021).

Table 1.4

Implementation and Enactment Curriculum Development Approaches (Synopsis of Sowell, 2000)

Implementation Approach	Enactment Approach
• Constitute curriculum committee for one academic subject (e.g., family studies or mathematics) and grade level within primary, junior (middle), and senior high levels. • Write the curriculum's vision statement with a rationale (why it is important that students learn *this* material in *this* way). • Specify educational philosophy(ies) underpinning the curriculum (see Table 1.1). • Develop educational aims (general end results) and then educational goals (specific end results). • Articulate learning objectives (cognitive, affective, psychomotor) and/or learning outcomes (competencies/skills) students must master often based on state, provincial, national, or disciplinary standards. • Drawing on may sources, select and tailor subject-matter and disciplinary content to specific grade levels; develop scope and sequence chart. • Explain expected/anticipated teaching methods (instructional strategies) and identify required or recommended materials and resources (usually teacher-centered learning). • Communicate the curriculum to the public and usually pilot test it with attendant revisions. • Publish final documents and provide to schools for implementation in concert with teacher professional development (PD) sessions and orientations. • Evaluate the process of developing the curriculum and evaluate the final product—*Are students learning what was intended and determined by others?* Caveat: this may not be what they *need* to learn or what they were *interested* in learning.	• Teachers (key curriculum planners) reflect on their own learnings and educational philosophy(ies) (see Table 1.1) *and* assess students' needs, strengths, and interests to determine what students need to learn. • Teachers develop a curriculum for their context (informed by Table 1.3) by designing learning experiences that teach students how to problem solve; engage in investigations and inquiry; and become proficient at being independent, self-regulated, self-directed learners. • Curricular content is based on themes (issues, important topics, problems, pressing matters, matters of interest) rather than subject matter, which *is* taught just not the same way. • Teach using an interdisciplinary, integrative approach using many types of knowledge and respecting many ways of knowing. • Rather than learning goals, teachers focus on the learning context (the physical setting, learning resources, and interpersonal relations) to ensure a student-centered learning environment. • Based on students' needs assessment, teachers select instructional strategies, resources, and learning materials so that students can choose and create their own activities, set their own learning pace in their chosen seating arrangements and groups; teachers scaffold student *enactment.* • Teachers attend to personal meaning (self and students') as authentic, organic curriculum evolves. • Teachers reflect on the process they used to enact the curriculum and then evaluate the final product—*How well did the curriculum meet students' needs and interests as identified through a needs assessment?*

Source: (Synopsis of Sowell, 2000).

Table 1.5

Kinds of Curriculum

Formal, Explicit, Overt, Official What is *supposed* to be taught	**Societal** What students learn via socializing forces outside of school
Pragmatic (Curriculum in Use) What is *actually* taught	**Concomitant/Home and Family** What students learn at home and in their family
Unofficial What teachers believe ought to be taught	**Rhetorical** Rhetoric from stakeholders outside the education system that affects curricula
Received (Learned) What students *actually* learn and understand (tested and verified)	**Phantom (Media Exposure)** Persistent messaging from mainstream media exposure that enculturates students to society's dominant views and to generational subcultures
Concealed, Internal Schema Learning in students' minds that is concealed from teachers (not tested or empirically verified)	**Electronic** What students learn on the internet and through social e-networking
Hidden, Covert, Implied Strong, enduring educational ideologies and social norms that students learn without realizing it (not formally taught or critically analyzed)	**Null** What is not taught (what is *left out* of student learning, intentionally or not)
Social What students learn when interacting with peers	

Source: Wilson (2021).

PREPARING AN EDUCATIONAL PHILOSOPHICAL STATEMENT

As noted, every educator has a philosophy of education—whether they know it or not (Petronicolos, 2011). This philosophy is influenced by personal experience, educational philosophies, curriculum theories, and approaches to developing curriculum. Lewis (2020) advised preparing a written educational philosophy statement that would contain a teacher's "most personal thoughts and beliefs on education" (para. 2). Such written statements help educators procure, organize, interpret, and then apply information gained from others and from self-reflection to make pedagogical decisions and take actions about and in learning environments (Boggs, 1981; Hitch & Youatt, 1995).

To facilitate this philosophical exercise, Lewis (2020) and Ornstein (1991) tendered a collection of questions to pose and ponder as one attempts to articulate and prepare an educational philosophical statement (see Table 1.6). Answering these questions helps PSTs and novice teachers locate themselves in relation to particular educational philosophies (see Table 1.1) that inform their "core beliefs about the purpose, process, nature, and ideals of education" (Petronicolos, 2011, p. 1).

Table 1.6

Questions to Help Shape Personal Educational Philosophical Statement

In my opinion:

(a) what is the greater purpose of education in society;

(b) what is the teacher's role;

(c) what role should students have in deciding what is learned and how;

(d) what should students learn about and why (e.g., knowledge, skills, processes, dispositions, principles, ideologies, norms, values, and beliefs);

(e) how do students learn best; and

(f) what is the best way to assess if they have learned anything?

Once written, this philosophical statement "inspires and directs educational planning, programs and processes in any given setting" (Lambert, 2017, para. 7). The document is normally two or three pages in length (Petronicolos, 2011) and is organic, meaning it is a living thing, changing and evolving with experience, new knowledge, and self-reflection. Educators should (a) continually reexamine their educational beliefs; (b) habitually reflect on their practices and actions; (c) constantly ponder what counts as education, teaching, and learning; and (d) regularly question their ideas about education, society, and learning (Lambert, 2017; Okoro, 2006; Petronicolos, 2011).

CHAPTER 2

DEVELOPING COURSE OUTLINES, MODULES, AND UNITS

It is imperative that PSTs and novice teachers know how to create new and revise existing course outlines, which also involves developing course modules and course units. Prowess with this skill set will serve them well into their career and can bring respect and high regard from school administrators, colleagues, parents, and guardians, even students.

DEVELOPING COURSE OUTLINES

A curriculum is prescriptive (should, ought to, judgmental). A course outline or syllabus is descriptive (describes without judgement). Although the terms are often interchanged, a course *syllabus* (i.e., a planning tool for a course of study) is technically more detailed than a course *outline* (i.e., a general plan showing essential features but few details). That said, both terms are used interchangeably herein as is the common convention. The outline (layout) for a specific course contains three main features with varying degrees of detail for each one (Altman & Cashin, 1992; Bain, 2004; Gannon, 2018; Posner & Rudnitsky, 2001):

a. *course information*—course name and number, grade level, year and months offered, meeting times and places, school identity, instructor information, course description, course Moodle, learning goals and learning objectives, topics, required texts and

Learning to Teach: Primer on Teacher Education Methods, pp. 19–34
Copyright © 2024 by Information Age Publishing
www.infoagepub.com

readings (organized into modules and units), materials required, assignments (details and due dates), and an evaluation scheme;

b.   *expectations of students*—attendance and lateness policies; course policies and procedures; late, incomplete, or missed-work policies; technology usage; inclusion and accessibility; classroom rules and etiquette; laboratory or gymnasium safety; and

c.   *school policies*—dress codes; codes of conduct; discipline guidelines; attendance and truancy; cell phone and computer technology usage; bullying and fighting; inclement weather; academic misconduct (dishonesty, cheating, plagiarism); and available support services.

Build Course Outline From Scratch

Posner and Rudnitsky (2001) developed a comprehensive approach to developing a course outline from scratch. They provided a 36-step process that is summarized in Table 2.1 and in the following narrative, which is prepared in second person (*you*) point of view to make the protracted and fleshed-out message more personable and immediately accessible.

Table 2.1

Major Steps to Create a Course Outline From Scratch

(a) get oriented (gain familiarity with state curricula, available textbooks, others' course outlines, and standards and outcomes' documents);

(b) set a direction (map out a draft, tentative plan);

(c) develop a course rationale (why it is important that students learn *this* content in *this* way);

(d) develop and then refine the Intended Learning Outcomes (ILOs) (using all (3) domains of Bloom's taxonomy);

(e) cluster the ILOs to form units (their term for modules);

(f) organize the units (include scope and sequence); and

(g) develop general teaching and instructional strategies (i.e., plan the learning environment and select strategies [methods] to deliver daily lessons and assess/evaluate learning).

Source: Extracted from Posner and Rudnitsky (2001).

In more detail, Posner and Rudnitsky's (2001) recommended first step is to describe the course in a paragraph. At the same time, you must become familiar with current curricular approaches to the subject matter (e.g., textbooks, curriculum documents, other people's course outlines). Next, create a list of any and all ideas (don't hold back) about what you think should be covered in the course. This can be in the form of words, phrases, and sentences. Now, try to find themes within that list. Themes comprise fragmented ideas that have meaning when brought together (Aronson, 1994). Some people find it useful to graph or concept map these ideas so they can see the connections among them. As your insights percolate, start playing around with titles for the course (unless the title is predetermined).

Drawing on this preliminary work, develop a tentative outline containing the main topics and subtopics you deem relevant and their envisioned sequence. But do not make any final decisions on exact content at this stage. This is still a work in progress. And, obviously, the less you know about a subject matter, the more work is involved at this stage. Once the tentative outline is teased out, it is time to shift gears and begin to map out intended learning outcomes (ILOs) (Posner & Rudnitsky, 2001).

Intended learning outcomes are predetermined by curriculum planners or teachers and spell out ahead of time what students are *supposed* to learn from the course—what you planned or meant (intended) the students to learn. This OBE approach is an example of a top-down curriculum. Enacted curricula do not start off with predetermined outcomes. In the top-down approach, educators may *intend* students to learn certain (a) facts, concepts, and ideas; (b) skills, techniques, competencies, and processes; (c) points of view, values, attitudes, and perspectives; or (d) emotions and feelings (rather than just knowledge per se) (Rao, 2020). Posner and Rudnitsky (2001) advised that teaching strategies, materials, and resources are not a concern at this stage, but you may want to start jotting these down to use later.

They proposed that, at this stage, you should be getting to the heart of the course – the "*Now* I know what this course will be about." This will be an "*A-ha!*" moment when everything becomes crystal clear. With this *clarity*, your next step is to determine the central (broad) questions of the course, questions that normally deal with some combination of six aspects of learning: (a) gaining knowledge and understanding; (b) gaining appreciation (e.g., taste, art, aesthetics); (c) problem solving; (d) decision making; (e) skills acquisition; or (f) personal growth and development. They cautioned that having too many broad questions at this stage means your course is still not focused enough—you need more clarity (Posner & Rudnitsky, 2001).

Posner and Rudnitsky (2001) recommended several strategies to help further refine and zone in on the true nature of the course (i.e., the central questions): (a) tease out the key building blocks of the course (concepts) and create a concept map, (b) write a story about the themes and how they are interrelated or (c) create a flow chart illustrating the complex arrangement of course elements. If not done already, you should determine students' existing knowledge and background about this subject matter (perhaps check scope and sequence charts from related courses and curricula), and then revise the original ILOs to reflect this assessment.

Although this next part usually appears at the beginning of the course outline, now is the time to attempt to write a rationale for the course. The rationale (i.e., logical set of reasons) will contain the purpose of the course and clarify why it is important that students learn what is in the course. *"What is the value gained from completing the course? What would happen if students did not learn this material?"* You can use this rationale to deal with government, media, principal, department head, parent/guardian even student's questions about why this course is needed. Unfortunately, this step is rarely taken because it entails delving into educational philosophies that concern the connection between learning, education, and society ... and many teachers are simply not philosophically savvy (McGregor, 2019).

Next, Posner and Rudnitsky (2001) recommended revising the ILOs again but this time using Bloom's (1956) taxonomy of learning (cognitive, affective, and psychomotor domains) with attendant learning verbs (see also Bloom et al., 1956; Krathwohl et al., 1964). The cognitive domain of learning pertains to the storage of information and knowledge in the brain. Affective learning relates to self-growth and interaction with others. The psychomotor domain deals with physical movement and perception (Anderson & Krathwohl, 2001; Bloom et al., 1956) (see Chapter 3).

You are now at the stage where you can prioritize this roster of ILOs and divide them into three piles: (a) students cannot leave the course without them, (b) they are important but not of the highest priority and (c) they are trivial (of little value or importance) and can be let go. Do this while you think about the central (broad-nature) questions of the course, the course description, its rationale, and any organizational aids and strategies you have created (e.g., flow charts, concept maps, narratives). You now have the fundamental bare bones of the course outline: name, description, rationale, and a collection of intended learning outcomes. The next step is to take these ideas and organize them into modules and units (Posner & Rudnitsky, 2001) (to be discussed later in this chapter).

Over the span of 25 years, I developed a course outline model for PSTs to use (see Table 2.2, which should be read in its entirety). My approach supplements Posner and Rudnitsky's (2001) model and also includes many ideas from Gross Davis (1999) plus my personal experience. PSTs and novice teachers are encouraged to move through the process set out in Table 2.2 and tick off ✓ each box as they complete the lesson-planning process, which is not as linear as it first appears. The text following Table 2.2 provides details on particular parts of the process that are not self-explanatory, self-evident, or sufficiently described in Table 2.2: (a) course rationale; (b) course aims, goals, and objectives; and (c) course organizational logic.

Table 2.2

Step-by-Step Course Outline Development Model

- Provide basic information (school's name, instructor's name and contact information, course name, grade level, classroom number, course Moodle URL if relevant and so on).
- Identify any prerequisites so students or parents/guardians can access students' readiness for the course.
- Provide course rationale and course description (i.e., respectively, justify content and pedagogy, and show how the course fits into the curriculum or a larger program of study).
- State both course goals (end point) and general student learning objectives (steps to get there)
- Clarify logic used to organize the course, sometimes called the course's conceptual framework (e.g., this could be a textbook's table of contents, moving from theory to application, from abstract to concrete, or moving through increased levels of complexity).
- Describe intended teaching approaches (i.e., instructional strategies) (e.g., lecture, labs, field trips, role playing, games, simulations).
- Specify text(s) and readings (where located) and whether mandatory or optional. Try to have a range of readings (e.g., texts, articles, web pages, popular press).
- Identify items students will need (e.g., laptop, flash drives, lab coat, binders, notebooks, folders, pens, highlighters, calculators, geometry kit).
- Provide an evaluation scheme. List assignments, tests, exams and such with dates and weights (value %). Explain grading practices and any scales/rubrics. Give students some sense of the workload required to complete course components (e.g., time, level of difficulty, solitary, or teamwork).
- Specify any other course requirements aside from in-class attendance (e.g., field trips, service learning, community engagement, exchange programs, learning abroad).
- Set out the course modules and units in detail (e.g., a schedule of classes displayed using a chart or table) with dates for each class including topics, readings, deadlines, holidays, due dates, drop dates.
- Clarify how the modules and units fit together as a whole so students can *see* the course in its entirety.
- Outline course policies and any relevant school policies (e.g., attendance, late assignments, makeups) including expected behavior before, during, and after class.

Course Rationale

Each teacher holds certain beliefs (examined or not) about education, learning, and society (Ornstein, 1991; Sowell, 2000). These beliefs are inherently reflected in their course-design decisions and inform any course rationale. A rationale is a set of reasons for taking a course of action (i.e., a logical basis for doing something) (Anderson, 2014). This reasoning can be used to justify why students must take a particular course and learn specific content in certain ways. Rationales stave off impressions that what is taught is simply expedient (i.e., advisable on practical rather than justifiable grounds). PSTs and novice teachers can use the rationale to address push back and challenges from people who do not understand why a particular approach is being used or content and processes are being taught (Brown, 1994). Drawing on the rationale, educators can better explain why the course is important and significant to students and society.

Beyond justifying the course to others, "the rationale serves as a guide and a check for all later steps in course planning" (Posner & Rudnitsky, 2001, p. 77). A rationale statement should begin with the subject matter to be addressed in the course as well as clarification of what the course is *not* about. Rationales should have reasons for including both the learning outcomes and the methods and procedures used to teach. "A well-articulated rationale will identify the expectations (roles) of teachers and learners and it should attempt to describe what the learners are like – their needs, interests, abilities, and challenges. And, if relevant, the rationale should relate learnings to social responsibilities, societal constraints or both" (McGregor, 2019, p. 4) (see Figure 2.1).

Figure 2.1

Sample Course Rationale

Food and Nutrition Grade 8 **Course Rationale**

Obesity and weight concerns are a pressing issue in North America. And there is a growing trend of individuals and families dining out, eating less-than-nutritious foods, and not learning basic cooking skills. This course is designed to orient Grade 8 students to the complex world of food and nutrition. The course serves as a general rather than comprehensive overview of the subject. Without this early understanding, students run the risk of making uncritical food and nutrition choices into their adulthood thereby perpetuating both the obesity epidemic and the inability to prepare healthy meals within their own life or home. This eventuality jeopardizes their health (and that of their family) and imposes heavy costs on governments and society. Upon completing the course in a collaborative learning environment (e.g., lectures, laboratory work, active learning), students will have gained fundamental knowledge, skills, and attitudes necessary to (a) choose and purchase healthy food, (b) make and prepare basic healthy meals and (c) begin to appreciate food as it pertains to their immediate and long-term health and nutritional well-being.

Course Aims, Goals, and Objectives

PSTs and novice teachers must specify the course aims, goals, and objectives, so they can use these when they create modules, units, and lesson plans. As with other terms related to educational initiatives, people mix up and interchange these three terms. Even dictionaries use them to define each other (see Anderson, 2014). Technically, a *course aim* is a statement indicating the course's general direction or overall intent. It is also an organizational principle, meaning it is a central reference point, a core assumption, from which everything else by proximity can derive meaning and value (Rider & Simmons, 2018; Wilson, 2021). This "everything else" includes course goals, objectives, and learning outcomes.

Course goals are also broad, but they are more specific than course aims. Goals are a desired end with no particular timeline (deadline). They are set for a reason, a purpose—goals serve to keep learning focused and on track. They tend to be long term in that they provide an end to strive for while in the course. *Course objectives* narrow things down even more to achievable, measurable outcomes. Objectives are precise and attainable in the short term. Simply put, incremental achievement of course objectives moves learners closer to reaching the course goals and keeps them travelling in the general direction of the course aims (Kumar, 2011; Wilson, 2021) (see Table 2.3).

Table 2.3

Examples of Course Aims, Goals, and Objectives

Course Aim Intended General *Direction* and an Organizational Principle	**Course Goal** More Specific *Intention*	**Course Objective** Very Specific *Outcome*
Students will understand and become proficient in identifying the different types of spoken English.	Students will be able to identify and use slang terms and phrases spoken in the United States.	Cognitive: Each student will identify and list five American slang terms he or she has heard from their peers.
		Affective: Students will justify their personal choice of three of the most offensive American slang terms from a list developed by the class.

Source: Extrapolated from Wilson, (2021).

Course Organizational Logic

Gross Davis (1999) recommended that teachers clarify the logic they used to organize their course content. Logic is Greek *logike tekhne*, "the art of reasoning" (Harper, 2022). In this instance, *reasoning* pertains to the power of the human mind to think, understand, form, and articulate judgements (i.e., qualified opinions). Logic is a reasoning system—a set of principles that underlie the arrangement of the elements of one's reasoning system (Anderson, 2014). To illustrate, the Preface set out the logic that I used to write this primer. Gross Davis (1999) identified a full range of logics relevant to organizing course material (see Table 2.4 listed in no particular order).

Table 2.4

Possible Logics to Organize Course Content

1. By topic or category
2. From concrete to abstract ideas
3. From abstract to concrete ideas
4. From theory to application
5. From application to theory
6. By increasing level of skill or complexity
7. How major concepts and their relationships are organized in the discipline
8. How students learn (learning styles and learning preferences)
9. How students develop competencies (prerequisite, novice, expert)
10. How knowledge has been created in the discipline or field of practice (present the evolution of conceptual, theoretical, and pragmatic innovations)
11. How students will use the information in their lives—in social, personal, or career settings
12. Chronological (e.g., good approach for a history or an archeology course)
13. Macro to micro (learn about a large phenomenon or establish a broad, general knowledge base and then shift to details of certain aspects, specific events, or concerns)
14. Proximal or distal: (a) begin by presenting an immediate, urgent problem (proximal—close proximity), and then explore its origins (distal—distance) or (b) begin by describing a phenomenon's origins, heritage, and context (distal), and then explore the relevancy of a topic in today's context (proximal)
15. Phenomenon or structure: respectively, (a) focus on description and analysis of specific works, events, and people in their *unique* settings or (b) emphasize description and analysis of *universal* theories, themes, and applications

Update or Adapt an Existing Course Outline

Sometimes, PSTs and novice teachers will be asked to teach a course for which there is an existing course outline. They may (a) have taught it before themselves, (b) be inheriting someone else's course or (c) be asked to use one created or imposed by the school board or state.

Update Course Taught Before

If they have taught the course before, teachers are encouraged to pull together everything they already have or can find on the course: old outlines, textbooks, handouts, notes, learning assignments, exams and, if available, students' feedback. Add to this any information and resources recently gathered from the evolving field, colleagues, and one's own changing knowledge base and interests. Use this collection of information to redesign the course (see Table 2.2) bearing in mind other constraints that may affect the revision process since it was last taught: hours available for the course, number of students, concurrent obligatory courses students must take, teacher's own evolving responsibilities and obligations, technological advances, available resources, and political will (Gross Davis, 1999).

Adapt an Inherited or Imposed Course Outline

If the PST or novice teacher is inheriting someone else's course, the first obvious step before adapting the course is to talk with that person(s) if still accessible. Also, if possible, ask for and obtain everything that person used to teach the course (see above) especially the course outline itself. Query them about any instructional difficulties they encountered, or problems students had when learning the content relative to how they taught the course. Would the previous teacher change or do anything differently? If that person is not available, use or adapt the course outline provided from the department head, school principal, or school board (Gross Davis, 1999). When adapting an inherited or imposed course, PSTs and novice teachers are encouraged to follow guidelines for developing a course from scratch (see Table 2.2) or redesigning a course they have taught before—in effect, draw on anything that helps them improve the inherited or imposed course outline for the new context.

DEVELOPING COURSE MODULES AND UNITS

A course outline is broken down into modules, and units. A recurring challenge that I faced when teaching PSTs was explaining how *module* and *unit* differ because these terms are often conflated (combined into one) or used interchangeably creating much confusion. Technically, a unit is an *individual* thing regarded as single and complete. A module is a *set of units* that can be used to construct a more complex structure (Anderson, 2014) such as a course. What matters is the principle that a module is the larger entity comprising smaller entities (units), which are subdivisions of the module. To mitigate confusion, for now, PSTs are advised to focus on discerning these two course organizational elements (i.e., a large structure with smaller structures nested in it) instead of worrying about what they are called per se.

Most courses contain two or three titled modules (lasting months or several weeks) each with several titled units (lasting a few weeks or several days) (Posner & Rudnitsky, 2001). Table 2.5 showcases the model that I developed to help PSTs with this aspect of course outline development. Please read Table 2.5 in its entirety because following this protocol will help ensure the careful and comprehensive creation of course modules and units. As with course outlines, PSTs and novice teachers are encouraged to move through the process and tick off ✓ each box □ as they complete it, appreciating that the process is not as linear as it first appears. It is an organic (alive) and iterative (back-and-forth) process whereby ongoing tweaks and improvements unfold over time *until* the PST or novice teacher is satisfied with the result and moves on to develop daily lesson plans. To clarify, Table 2.5 works best with the implementation, top-down approach.

Table 2.5

Process for Developing Course Modules and Units

Each *module* (usually 2–3 per course) is organized around a theme, issue, or problem that represents a key (broad) building block of the course. The module can also correspond to a chapter topic in a textbook or ideas from standards and outcomes' documents for the area of study.

□ Give each module a title reflecting the broad topic being covered.

□ Review state (provincial, national, territorial) and disciplinary guidelines and approved textbooks for age-appropriate content and tasks for this area of study. Then, align each module with previously articulated course goal(s) and develop intended learning objectives (ILOs).

□ Decide on the sequence of the modules (i.e., the order they will be taught) using organizational logic (see Table 2.4), tips from textbooks, or existing arrangements in curricular documents.

□ Now, break each module down into manageable *units*, usually 2–3 per module, with 2–3 lesson plans per unit, tentatively deciding on their sequence as well.

□ Identify relevant content, materials, and resources that are necessary to implement the modules and units. Gather information from a variety of perspectives and sources about the course's main building blocks. Create a filing system for the course. One approach is to use a file folder (literal or virtual) for each module and perhaps each unit and even lessons within units. Print and file the information as you find it, so you can easily add to it, keep it organized and current, and access it (paper based in file cabinet or virtual, e.g., Pinterest).

□ When satisfied that you have the scope and depth needed to teach the topic, create a narrative (like a term paper) for each unit (about five typed, single-spaced pages). Once completed, begin to convert this information into PowerPoints, Visme, Prezi, Genially, slides, overheads, handouts et cetera, if you are ready to distill it this far. This will become the content that you eventually teach in each daily lesson. This content is organic. It is an alive document—a work in progress that you must perpetually keep current.

□ Now that you know better what is going to be taught, decide on the time frame required for each module and unit. For modules, divide the number of weeks for the course by the number of modules to get an estimate (12 weeks/4 modules = 3 weeks per module). Decide how many classes (days, lessons) are required for each unit within each module.

□ Next, create a day-to-day timeline of each unit's activities and daily lessons dependent on the number of classes per week. Using the information pulled together so far, block out a series of daily lessons that are representative of important elements of the unit and progressive in nature—a flow chart works here. When more detail is needed, follow guidelines for developing detailed lesson plans (see Chapter 3).

□ Develop a plan to assess and evaluate learning at the end of each module (i.e., at the end of each 3–4 weeks). If the module has a culminating activity (e.g., midterm, term paper, laboratory session, project) that represents assessment of its learning goals, this activity should be clearly described in the course outline. The same rule applies for units, if relevant.

Posner and Rudnitsky (2001) clarified that there is no rule for how *big* a module (or a unit) should be (i.e., no magic number of ILOs, objectives, sessions, classes, or lessons). To decide a module's size, educators can take guidance from two principles: (a) *scope* (what will be covered in the course) and (b) *coherence* (i.e., logical agreement among the parts covered in the course). Regarding *scope*, the modules and units should encompass everything that the PST or novice teacher deemed relevant to the course as articulated in the course rationale, aims, goals, and objectives. A manageable, *coherent* module will be readily seen as a set of learnings (units) that relate to each other. To that end, the subject matter covered in the course should be broken into parts that can then be joined with other parts, so students can *see* the *whole* picture including how the modules fit together to complete the *course's* aims, goals, and objectives (Posner & Rudnitsky, 2001).

Figure 2.2 provides an example of the modules and units for my 12-week university course (three hours per week) on *Curriculum Practices in Family Studies II*. Bolded text in the objectives flags the course's key building blocks. Each titled module and unit targets specific building blocks. Care was taken to ensure that students in the course could readily *see* the connection between the course's rationale and objectives (really, course aims per Wilson's, 2021, distinction) and the modules and units comprising the course. This transparency helped them better appreciate *why* they were learning what they were learning in that particular sequence as they prepared to be a full-fledged teacher.

An even more detailed illustration of modules and units is provided in Table 2.6 for a Grade 8 *Food and Nutrition* course, which contains five course objectives: (a) develop skills for food safety, preparation, and handling while working in food-lab groups; (b) demonstrate an understanding of the relationship between nutrient intake and health; (c) implement responsible food resource management practices; (d) develop a rudimentary understanding of the psychology of food; and (e) identify locally produced food products and, at a novice level, discern their importance in the local economy. There are four modules and nine units in total in which all five course objectives are targeted with some objectives receiving more treatment than others per the course rationale.

Different from Figure 2.2, Table 2.6 is further broken down into daily lessons, attendant readings, and relevant assessment and evaluation. This 12-week course has four, 30-minute classes each week, totaling 48 classes. Although it may seem like too much time is allowed for some topics, flexibility is built in for run-over time or less time than needed to teach particular lessons. Students use a textbook titled *Food for Life* (Witte, 2008). Formative (ongoing) assessment and summative (warp-up) evaluation for this course entails (a) two tests (20%); (b) learning activities and assignments (reflections, lab reports, in-class activities—each with its own rubric) (60%); and (c) lab participation and group work (also with rubrics) (20%).

Figure 2.2

Example of Course Modules and Units

EDUC 5386 *Curriculum Practices in Family Studies II*

Course Rationale

To be effective and responsible educators, preservice teachers must appreciate the larger philosophical and theoretical context within which teaching occurs and course development and delivery unfold. This course answers the question *"How do I prepare an entire course and attendant modules and units couched in existing provincial curricula that are informed by educational philosophies?"* This process involves familiarity with (a) dominant educational philosophies and curriculum orientations; (b) curriculum development models (implementation and enactment); and (c) theory about how to develop course outlines, modules, and units. What to do before, during, and after a lesson was covered in the prerequisite course (EDUC 5385 *Curriculum Practices in Family Studies I*).

Course Objectives:

- To gain critical understandings of the basic **educational philosophies,** over 10 **curriculum orientation** perspectives, and over 10 **kinds of curriculum** (e.g., null, explicit, hidden);
- To gain detailed understanding of steps involved in **curriculum development** (includes philosophical rationale, scope, and sequence) and each of **implementation** (top-down) **and enactment** (bottom-up) models; and
- To fully understand and then apply theory related to **developing curriculum products:** how to **create course outlines, modules,** and **units.**

Modules and Units

This 12-week course has two modules (with two units each) that are aligned with the above numbered course objectives.

MODULE ONE (6 weeks): Educational Philosophies, Curriculum Orientations, Curriculum Development

Unit 1.1 Educational Philosophies and Curriculum Orientations (course objective 1) (4 weeks)

- Develop a critical understanding of both educational philosophies and curriculum orientations. *"What is the curriculum? What is knowledge? What should students be learning? Who should decide what should be taught? How are such decisions to be made?"*

Unit 1.2 Curriculum Development (course objective 2) (2 weeks)

- Gain a deep appreciation for the processes, strategies, and approaches to designing (developing) new curricula and redesigning existing curricula.

MODULE TWO (6 weeks): Curriculum Products: Course Outlines, Modules, and Units

Unit 2.1 Course Outline Design (course objective 3) (3 weeks)

- Design a complete course from the provincial family studies curriculum and include both modules and units.

Unit 2.2 Module and Unit Design (course objective 3) (3 weeks)

- From the above course, choose one module and create its supportive units including all content to be taught (no lesson plans are required for this assignment).

To be discussed in Chapter 3, there are three main domains of learning (cognitive, affective, and psychomotor) each with several levels of learning (Anderson & Krathwohl, 2001). PSTs and novice teachers can confine each module to one domain of learning (e.g., psychomotor), but it is acceptable to mix several learning domains in one module (Posner & Rudnitsky, 2001). Using Table 2.6 as an example, Unit 4.1 combines cognitive with psychomotor while Unit 3.2 combines cognitive and affective. Unit 1.3 is focused on just the cognitive domain.

Table 2.6

Detailed Modules and Units for a Grade 8 Food and Nutrition Course

Grade 8 Food and Nutrition: *It's All About Food*		
This introductory Food and Nutrition course was developed from the scientific study of nutrition and food science. Students will learn to understand the relation between nutrition, foods, and health by studying nutrition as well as learning how to make informed food choices, safely and correctly prepare foods, and follow basic recipes. To a lesser extent, the course investigates the psychology of food, provincial local food products, global food issues, and food-related careers. The intent is for teenage students to better situate themselves in their local and global food environment. The course will be taught using a combination of in-class theory and assignments, at-home readings, reflections, and hands-on laboratory sessions.		
Week and Learning Objective	**Topics and Learning Activities**	**Textbook Readings (examples)**
MODULE 1: Healthy Food-Happy Body (4 units)		
Week 1 (Four 30–min classes) Learning Objective 4	**Unit 1.1 Introduction** Welcome class. Complete and submit student information sheets. Review course outline and class expectations. Ice breaker game: Pick a food, introduce yourself, and explain why that food. Complete Personal Quiz: *Do I Think I Eat Healthy?* Then, respectfully discuss answers in class.	Homework reading (16 pages): 1–9, 13–15, 18, 20–21
Week 2 (Four 30–min classes) Learning Objectives 2 and	**Unit 1.2 Canada's Food Guide** Introduce *Canada's Food Guide* Complete food guide exploration activity (2–3 classes) Personal Reflection: In 3–5 sentences, explain how you think healthy food choices affect your health today and tomorrow (submit in class).	Homework reading (5 pages): 312–316

(Table continued on next page)

Table 2.6 (Continued)

Detailed Modules and Units for a Grade 8 Food and Nutrition Course

Week 3 (Four 30–min classes) Learning Objective 2	Unit 1.3 Healthy Food Choices Return students' reflections. PowerPoint on how healthy food choices affect people's present and future health. Expose students to complex concept of nutrients. Food label activity.	Homework reading (19 pages): 62–79, 83
Week 4 (Four 30–min classes) Learning Objective 2	Unit 1.4 Food Label and Nutrient Analysis Correct food label activity from last class. Carrousel activity: Compare and contrast nutrient content of various foods. Write and then submit reflections on Unit 1. Prepare and review for first test (Module 1's content).	
MODULE 2: Let's Get Cooking Part A (2 units)		
Week 5 (Four 30–min classes) Learning Objective 1	Unit 2.1 Safety during Food Preparation Return students' reflections. Administer first test (Module 1's content). Begin to read and fill out teacher-provided protocol sheets on (a) safe work habits in the kitchen and (b) proper use of food appliances and cooking equipment. Provide overview of how to follow a recipe.	
Week 6 (Four 30–min classes) Learning Objective 1	Unit 2.1 Safety during Food Preparation (continued) Return first test. Video demonstrating safe work habits in the kitchen and proper use of kitchen tools and equipment. Video showing appropriate techniques for measuring liquid and dry ingredients. Complete and review last week's kitchen safety and protocol sheets.	Homework reading (10 pages): 230–239
Week 7 (Four 30–min classes) Learning Objective 1	Unit 2.2 Food Preparation Experience First food laboratory experience. Prepare and submit lab report and self-reflection on lab experience.	Homework reading (14 pages): 307–312, 366–367

(Table continued on next page)

Table 2.6 (Continued)

Detailed Modules and Units for a Grade 8 Food and Nutrition Course

MODULE 3: Me, My World, and Food (2 units)		
Week 8 (Four 30–min classes) Learning Objective 5	**Unit 3.1 Nova Scotia Food Products and Related Industries** Return lab reports and reflections. Quest speaker on Nova Scotia egg production. Quest speaker on NS salmon farming and/or blueberry farming. Guidance counselor on food-related careers. Class debriefing. Write and submit reflections on local food industries and career options.	
Week 9 (Four 30–min classes) Learning Objective 3	**Unit 3.2 The Food Consumer and the Power of Food** Return students' reflections. Students personally read sections of textbook in class. Facilitate discussion of in-class readings about the power of food. Complete activity: *How does my environment affect the way I eat?* Briefly discuss consumer behavior decisions involved in food purchasing. Prepare and submit reflections on "The Food Consumer."	In-class, 9-page reading: 298–306 Homework reading (15 pages): 10–12, 26–37
Week 10 (Four 30–min classes) Learning Objective 4	**Unit 3.2 The Food Consumer and the Power of Food (continued)** Return students' reflections on "The Food Consumer." Teacher-facilitated discussion of homework readings on global and local food issues and food as a social, emotional, cultural, and an economic experience. Prepare and submit reflections on "The Power of Food."	

(Table continued on next page)

Table 2.6 (Continued)

Detailed Modules and Units for a Grade 8 Food and Nutrition Course

MODULE 4: Let's Get Cooking Part B (1 unit)		
Week 11 (Four 30–min classes) Learning Objective 1	**Unit 4.1 Food Preparation Basics/Experience** Return students' reflections on "The Power of Food." Second food laboratory experience. Prepare and submit lab report and self-reflections on this lab. Administer second test—Module 3's content	
Week 12 (Four 30–min classes) Learning Objective 1	**Unit 4.1 Food Preparation Basics/Experience (continued)** Return test, lab reports, and lab reflections. Third food laboratory experience. Fourth food laboratory experience. For each lab, prepare and submit lab reports and self-reflections on the labs. **Last class** wrap up (return lab reports and reflections).	

CHAPTER 3

BEFORE CLASS

Learning Styles, Learning Objectives, Lesson Plans, and Learning Environments

The *before-class* time frame pertains to any work PSTs and novice teachers do in preparation for meeting with students (in person or online) and teaching them. A lot of thinking and preparation goes into preparing a lesson *before* actually delivering it in class. This chapter concerns four topics in particular: (a) students' learning styles and learning preferences; (b) writing effective, measurable learning objectives; (c) preparing daily lesson plans; and (d) setting up the learning environment. Taken together, these four factors deeply shape students' learning experiences and their academic achievement.

STUDENTS' LEARNING STYLES AND LEARNING PREFERENCES

In the spirit of a primer, this section presents a sampling of reputable learning style theories as a way to sensitize PSTs and novice teachers to the stark yet beautiful reality that every student learns differently (Weston & Cranton, 1986). Each person has a dominant learning style(s). Style means a manner of doing something. In education, *style* refers to general intellectual functioning that differentiates one learner from another (Brown, 2000). Indeed, a *learning* style refers to how students learn *best*—how they perceive, gather, and process course-related information. Bottom line— one style of teaching will not reach all students. PSTs and novice teachers have to mix things up so that each lesson has something for everyone—can

Learning to Teach: Primer on Teacher Education Methods, pp. 35–65
Copyright © 2024 by Information Age Publishing
www.infoagepub.com

reach everyone. This is inherently challenging and time consuming but ultimately deeply rewarding.

Gardner's Multiple Intelligences

Not all students are *word smart* (learn verbally using language) or *number or logic smart* (mathematical, causation, reasoning) (Şener & Çokçaliskan, 2018). With this appreciation, Gardner (2008) coined the term *multiple intelligences* to convey the premise that people learn and understand things in a variety of ways. By *intelligences* (plural) he meant that the psychological construct of *intelligence* can be measured in ways other than (a) cognition (i.e., intelligence quotient [IQ] tests) or (b) psychology (i.e., personality tests). Table 3.1 summarizes Gardner's nine intelligences and pairs each with relevant learning verbs and outcomes (see also Carlson-Pickering, 1999; GP-Training, 2021; Şener & Çokçaliskan, 2018).

Table 3.1

Gardner's Nine Multiple Intelligences

Type of intelligence	Explanation (with possible career paths)	Learning Objective Verbs or Outcomes
Verbal-Linguistic (Word smart)	Can use language (spoken and written) to express your self, what is on your mind. Can comprehend others' words and thoughts and compose your own thoughts (e.g., teachers, journalists, lawyers, authors, researchers)	discuss, describe, articulate, summarize, paraphrase, interpret, debate, express, process
Logical-Mathematical (Number or logic smart)	Can logically (deductive logic) and systematically comprehend a situation, calculate, and analyze things, reason and problem solve, appreciate cause and effect, and see relationships and underlying principles (e.g., scientists, statisticians, engineers, accountants, mathematicians, computer programmers, network administrators)	analyze, experiment, classify, order, solve, abstract, plan, prioritize, calculate, predict, detect patterns, reason deductively, think logically, argumentation
Visual-Spatial (Picture smart)	Can see (visualize) the world *in your mind* and then represent that mind space in artwork, creative ventures, or images. Able to perceive, modify, and create images (e.g., artists, designers, architects, navigators)	conceptualize, imagine, see patterns, design, construct, diagram, sketch, visualize, map, perceive, create, puzzle solve, chart

(Table continued on next page)

Table 3.1 (Continued)

Gardner's Nine Multiple Intelligences

Type of intelligence	Explanation (with possible career paths)	Learning Objective Verbs or Outcomes
Bodily-Kinaesthetic (Body smart)	Tend to use your whole body to learn and express what you have learned. Move and use your body to solve problems, create products, or deliver services (e.g., athletes, dancers, mechanics, actors, firefighters, crafters)	manipulate, express, stretch, bend, perform, move, feel, gesture, flex, assemble, balance
Interpersonal (People smart)	Able to know about, understand, and work with others (their emotions, intentions, motivations, desires, beliefs) (e.g., therapists, counsellors, salespeople, hairdressers, talk-show hosts, political and community leaders)	counsel, interview, connect, join, empathize, interact, mediate, group learning, coordinate, collaborate
Intrapersonal (Self-smart)	Able to delve deeply into yourself and gain self-knowledge and insights (who you are, what you can do, your limits, aspirations); can interpret your own feelings, emotions, and motivations (e.g., poets, novelists, entrepreneurs, researchers, spiritual leaders)	reflect, meditate, ponder, sit, muse, contemplate, infer, introspect, self-assess, retreat
Existential (Life/big-picture smart)	Can comfortably ask the big questions about your existence as a human, death, the meaning of life, and the reason for your existence (e.g., theorists, philosophers, spiritual and religious leaders, some authors)	pose deep questions, ponder meanings, deeply understand, think philosophically, seek (un)truths
Musical/Rhythmic (Music smart)	Able to "think in music" (auditory learning, timing, rhythms, sounds, pitch, tones, notes) and hear, recognize, and maybe manipulate patterns; use music to say what you have to say and express what you have learned (e.g., musicians, singers, composers, disk jockeys, hip-hop artists)	harmonize/rhythms, synthesize, sing, play, listen, compose, record, orchestrate, vibrate, produce, direct, perform, reverberate
Naturalistic (Nature smart)	Able to readily order and classify aspects of nature; sensitive to features of the natural world, and you can distinguish people from nature while appreciating that they are interconnected (e.g., farmers, gardeners, botanists, environmentalists, astronomers, biologists)	balance, conserve, protect, order, advocate, observe, preserve, harmony, classify

Source: Gardner (2008).

Kolb's Learning Styles

Kolb (1984) developed learning styles based on how students prefer to take in and then process information. They may prefer to (a) *perceive and take in* information using (1) concrete experiences (senses, personal involvement, feelings) or (2) abstract conceptualizations (mentally visualize, analyze, theorize). They may prefer to (b) *process and internalize* that information to create new knowledge by (1) active experimentation (doing and applying) or (2) reflective observation (watching and pondering).

Kolb (1984) used these two strands to create four learning styles: (a) concrete experience (CE) (*do, act*); (b) reflective observation (RO) (*observe, watch*); (c) abstract conceptualization (AC) (*think, digest*); and (d) active experimentation (AE) (*plan, want*). In short, CEs learn by being involved in and reacting to new experiences. ROs learn by watching and listening to others and through self-observation. ACs learn by creating theories to explain what they have observed; they learn from thinking. AEs learn by using theories to problem solve, make decisions, and plan; they learn from the results emergent from planning, deciding, or solving something. More detail follows with examples of recommended instructional strategies.

Concrete Experience (CE)

Concrete experience learners learn by doing, by being involved. They relate well to people and learn by sharing ideas. They rely on their intuition and are sensitive to others' feelings. They need a teacher who motivates them, and they appreciate being told how what they are learning relates to their life. Effective instructional strategies include providing concrete examples and problem sets and arranging field trips, laboratories, and simulations (Anderson & Adams, 1992; Kolb, 1984).

Reflective Observers (RO)

Students learn best by watching and reflecting. They view things from different perspectives and look for meaning. They learn through perception and then reflection. They are interested in how things work but withhold judgement until careful observation and serious thought and consideration. Teachers should use journaling, logs, brainstorming, rhetorical questions (make a point instead of getting an answer), and thought-provoking questions (Anderson & Adams, 1992; Kolb, 1984).

Abstract Conceptualizers (AC)

Students learn best by logically analyzing ideas, systematically planning things, and acting on their intellectual understandings of a situation gained from thinking and digesting what and as they are learning. They thrive on theories, abstractions (ideas), and experts' opinions. They learn best from teachers who lecture and assume the role of expert by logically presenting organized facts and information with time allowed to ponder and consider. AC students learn best from model building, analogies (using comparisons to explain and clarify), and writing theoretical essays (Anderson & Adams, 1992; Kolb, 1984).

Active Experimenters (AE)

Students learn best through taking risks and planning. They like to be left on their own to (a) learn through trial and error (i.e., actively experiment with ideas) and (b) problem solve in a learning environment where the teacher scaffolds their learning but stays out of the way. Teachers are encouraged to use fieldwork, project-based learning (PBL), case studies, and laboratory work (Anderson & Adams, 1992; Kolb, 1984).

Gregorc's Learning Styles

Still concerned with how students take in and process information, Gregorc (1984) also created four learning styles by relying on concrete and abstract. But unlike (Kolb, 1984), Gregorc chose to combine these with students' two *ordering* abilities (i.e., making sense of what they have perceived): (a) random (unorganized, not systematic) or (b) sequential (organized, systematic). From Gregorc's perspective, *concrete* means "it is what it is." Students do not look for hidden meanings or relationships between ideas. *Abstract* is the opposite. Students seek meaning and implications and become aware of information by using intuition and imagination. *Sequential* means students must plan and use a step-by-step process in order to take in and process information. *Random* means students can learn (make sense of things) by ignoring order. They can start at the end or the beginning or even skip steps and still learn.

Using these distinctions, Gregorc (1984) formulated four learning styles. (a) *Concrete sequential* (CS) learners learn best from linear, step-by-step, ordered, and practical teaching. (b) *Concrete random* (CR) learners view learning as both intuitive and concrete. They are independent learners that thrive on problem solving and practical applications. (c) *Abstract sequential*

(AS) learners are analytical and thrive on mental challenges. They like things orderly, predictable, and logical and learn best in quiet but mentally stimulating environments. (d) *Abstract random* (AR) learners are imaginative, spontaneous, flexible, and emotional. They learn best in an informal, active learning environment where they can create mental, multidimensional webs of concepts and ideas that make sense to them.

McCarthy's Learning Styles

McCarthy (1980, 1990) created a simpler approach that is also based on how students perceive and then process course-related information. She called it the *4MAT* style using the neologism (newly coined word) as a play on words for *formatting* a lesson plan, so it accommodates all 4 learning styles. McCarthy differentiated each learning style by students' favorite (preferred) questions (ways of learning): (a) *Why?* (imaginative learner), (b) *What?* (analytical learner), (c) *How* does this work? (common sense learner) and (d) *What if?* (dynamic learner). Details follow with recommended teaching strategies.

Imaginative Learner (Why?)

In truth, the imaginative learner does not seem to be well named. Imaginative means having or showing inventiveness and creativity (Anderson, 2014). But McCarthy (1980, 1990) conceptualized these learners as needing to personally connect with the course material, so they can find personal meaning in it. They *need a reason* to learn it (a *Why?*). They are curious learners (thus the label *imagination?*). The information has to connect to their daily lives and personal experiences. Otherwise, it is hard for them to process it into new knowledge. The learning environment has to convey trust, involve personal interactions, and provide chances to listen and share ideas. Effective teaching strategies are cooperative learning, integrated curricula, thematic instruction, class discussions, case studies, and brainstorming.

Analytical Learner (What?)

Analytical learners are so named because they learn best by examining the elements or structure of something in detail. They seek continuity and certainty. Once information (facts, statistics, evidence, proof) is perceived, they process it by separating it into parts, thinking through their ideas, learning what the experts think, and then judging the information's accuracy. If they deem it worthy, they will internalize it as new knowledge (information is outside the brain, while knowledge is inside). This deepens their understandings of both concepts and processes being taught in the course. This way, they learn by answering *What?* Teachers should use lectures, guest experts, debates, essays, and provide chances to collect and analyze data and engage in independent research. Analytic learners enjoy ideas more than they do people (McCarthy, 1980, 1990).

Common Sense Learner (How?)

Common sense means using ordinary good sense (reason or purpose) and sound judgement in practical matters; it also means judging in a way that is *common* to others (Anderson, 2014). Common sense learners are level-headed, can assess a situation, and they learn by figuring out *how things work*. They also need to know that what they learn will be useful and practical. To help them figure this all out, teachers should provide opportunities for them to test their evolving understandings by creating, building, experimenting, and doing things (e.g., projects, practical demonstrations, field trips, and lab experiences). Theory is not enough for these learners. They need to test the theory using strategic thinking to see if it really works by using common sense. They also need an answer, so teachers must ensure closure (McCarthy, 1980, 1990).

Dynamic Learner (What If...?)

Dynamic learners learn best through discovery—"*What if* we did this?" Dynamic means full of energy and new ideas, always changing (Anderson, 2014). Dynamic learners access and process course-based information by using their intuition, embracing challenges, taking risks, and putting a new spin on things; they also learn by trial and error. They flourish in unstructured, independent study environments, and they learn best through role playing, games, simulations, drama, art projects, and creative writing—anything that involves discovery (i.e., finding things while searching). Teachers are facilitators (make learning easier) who are also comfortable letting dynamic learners teach other students (McCarthy, 1980, 1990).

Dunn and Dunn's Learning Preferences

Dunn and Dunn (1993) did not conceive of types of learning styles so much as they identified five dimensions (21 elements) along which students can have strong and weak *preferences* for learning: environmental, physiological, emotional, sociological, and psychological preferences (see Table 3.2, which should be read by rows, left to right) (see also American TESOL

Institute, 2011). A preference is a greater liking for one thing over others—something is preferable, desirable, considered suitable, a first choice, a natural inclination (Anderson, 2014). The learning-preference approach is useful for PSTs and novice teachers because it is a practical, nuts-and-bolts perspective that balances the more theoretical stances of the other learning style scholars profiled in this chapter that were based on how students perceive and then process information.

Table 3.2

Dunn and Dunn's (1993) Students' Learning Preferences

Dimensions (5)	Elements (21)			
Physical Environment	Light	Sound	Room temperature	Seating arrangements, floor plan, and furniture design
Physiological	Time of day and energy levels affect learning	Mobility (can learn sitting still or need to move to learn)	Intake to concentrate (need for food or to bite things [pens, pencils])	Perceptual strengths (senses used to learn): auditory, visual, tactile, reading and writing, or kinesthetic (whole-body movement)
Emotional	Motivation (learn to please parents or teachers)	Task persistence (finish completely or take breaks)	Conform or not to learning task (do what teacher says or not)	Structure of learning environment (need direction or can work alone)
Sociological —preferred learning relations	Self (alone)	Pairs	Peers Teams	Authoritative adults Varied
Psychological	Impulsive or reflective learner (response time): speak without thinking versus hold back for accuracy		Analytic or global learner: need details to learn versus can learn with big picture	Either left or right brain dominant (hemispheric): analytical/logical thinking or creative/ artistic thinking

Source: Dunn and Dunn (1993).

To wrap up this section on learning styles, it is imperative that PSTs and novice teachers gain an appreciation that students have different learning styles or particular strengths and preferences in the way they take in and process information.

> Some students tend to focus on facts, data, and algorithms; others are more comfortable with theories and mathematical models. Some respond strongly

to visual forms of information, like pictures, diagrams, and schematics; others get more from verbal forms—written and spoken explanations. Some prefer to learn actively and interactively; others function more introspectively and individually. (Felder, 1996, p. 18)

PSTs and novice teachers need to diligently accommodate learning styles and learning preferences to the best of their abilities using available resources.

WRITING LEARNING OBJECTIVES

With a better appreciation of the need to accommodate different learning styles and learning preferences, the discussion now turns to the skill of writing learning objectives that reflect this learning diversity. Top-down implementation curricula require predetermined, *intended* learning objectives (ILOs). This section (a) explains Bloom's (1956) taxonomy of learning and additional domains not addressed by Bloom; (b) differentiates between learning goals and learning objectives; and (c) concludes with guidelines for writing effective, measurable learning objectives. PSTs and novice teachers need to practice and learn this material before they can begin developing lesson plans (see next section) whose purpose is to help students achieve the intended learning objectives.

Bloom's Domains of Learning

In a top-down, implementation environment, PSTs and novice teachers will likely be expected to prepare their learning objectives using *verbs* indicative of Bloom's (1956) three domains of learning (i.e., cognitive, affective, and psychomotor). Although developed by several people over time (Anderson & Krathwohl, 2001; Bloom et al., 1956; Dave, 1970; Harrow, 1972; Krathwohl et al., 1964; Simpson, 1972), the convention is to simply say *Bloom's taxonomy*. The seminal originators, Bloom et al. (1956), used the term taxonomy (Greek *taxis*, "arrangement") for their approach, wherein they *classified* and then *arranged* learning into different categories (domains, in this case) and different levels in a particular order or sequence and then associated specific verbs with each level. A verb is word that describes an action to be taken (Anderson, 2014), in this case students' actions so they can learn the material.

Briefly, the mode of learning in the *cognitive* domain (six levels) is thinking and thoughts—mental operations used while learning. The *affective* domain (five levels) involves self-growth in emotions, feelings, and social connections arising from and instilled while learning. The *psychomotor* domain (five levels) concerns action and doing while concurrently using mental operations (cognitive). In the psychomotor domain, attendant gross and fine muscle skills and motor actions pertain to discrete physical functions, reflex actions, and interpretive movements (Wilder, 2019; Wilson, 2021). Table 3.3 provides an introductory overview to Bloom's taxonomy (Anderson & Krathwohl, 2001; Bloom et al., 1956; Dave, 1970; Krathwohl et al., 1964). Graphically, each learning domain (with its attendant levels) is often represented using a triangle (see Figure 3.1, Microsoft clipart used with permission).

Table 3.3

Overview of Revised Bloom's Taxonomy With Higher Order Skills on Top

Cognitive (knowledge/knowing/*head*)	Affective (attitude/feeling/*heart*)	Psychomotor (skills/doing/*hands*)
• creating (synthesis) • evaluating • analyzing • applying • understanding (comprehension) • remembering (knowledge)	• characterizing • organizing • valuing • responding • receiving	• naturalization • articulation • precision • manipulation • imitation

Figure 3.1

Triangular Representation of Bloom's Revised Cognitive Learning Domain

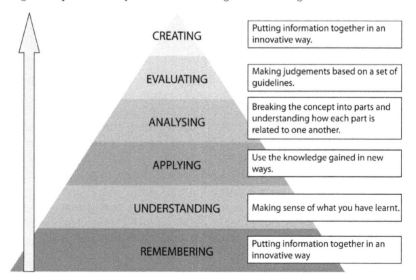

In more detail, a *domain* is a sphere of activity or knowledge. A *taxonomy* is hierarchical (ranked) and cumulative. This means that the lower levels within a specific learning domain require less ability (or a different ability) than the higher levels, and learning becomes more sophisticated often indicated with an upward pointing arrow (see Figure 3.1). Teachers' questions pertaining to each level within a domain require learners to respond using a different kind of thought process. If taught as intended, each level within a domain builds on the others thereby exposing learners to a variety of thought processes. But teachers can choose to teach at just one level of a domain if pedagogically justified (Cooper, 1986; Posner & Rudnitsky, 2001; Wilder, 2019) (e.g., just teach *remembering* within the cognitive domain, *valuing* in the affective domain, or *precision* in the psychomotor domain) (see Table 3.3).

Many teachers are choosing to use the *Revised Bloom's Taxonomy* (RBT) with changes made to the cognitive domain only; levels were renamed and reordered with nouns converted to verbs (Anderson & Krathwohl, 2001) (see Figure 3.1). Also, although Bloom and colleagues (1956) did not originally create subcategories for the psychomotor domain 65 years ago, three other educators did: Dave (1970), Harrow (1972), and Simpson (1972). Dave's (1970) approach was used in this chapter. Note that while the cognitive domain is the most familiar and common, students must learn across all three domains to ensure a holistic education and the development of the whole person (Fleck, 1980). Table 3.4 profiles the three domains of learning with associated verbs that PSTs and novice teachers can use when writing learning objectives and learning outcomes (Anderson & Krathwohl, 2001; Bloom et al., 1956; Dave, 1970; Krathwohl et al., 1964).

Table 3.4

Bloom's Taxonomy of Learning with Associated Verbs

Learning Domain and Respective Levels of Learning		Associated Verbs
Cognitive: intellectual aspect of learning; relates to information (outside the brain) and knowledge (stored in the brain) and to the intellectual abilities and skills to use both (six levels)		
Remembering (knowledge)	requires memory only; recall, retrieve, or recognize previously learned material that has been memorized or internalized in long-term memory and is consistent with presented material	define, identity, recall, list, recognize, select, locate, describe, repeat, recite, acquire, name, match

(Table continued on next page)

Table 3.4 (Continued)

Bloom's Taxonomy of Learning with Associated Verbs

Learning Domain and Respective Levels of Learning		Associated Verbs
Cognitive: intellectual aspect of learning; relates to information (outside the brain) and knowledge (stored in the brain) and to the intellectual abilities and skills to use both (six levels)		
Understanding (comprehension)	making sense (constructing meaning) of what has been learned (ideas, concepts, constructs); interpreting information in own words (rephrase, reword—express the same thing using different words and in alternative ways)	classify, categorize, infer, demonstrate, describe in own words, paraphrase, represent, translate, summarize, sort, discuss, compare, contrast, differentiate, extrapolate, explain in own words, infer, exemplify
Applying	practice using the knowledge in a familiar situation or in new ways or new situations	apply, construct, display, demonstrate, explain, use, operate, prepare, adapt, develop, extend, implement, practice, execute, carry out
Analyzing	breaking concepts into parts and understanding how the parts are related to each other and to the overall structure from which they came; identify motives and causes, determine evidence, and draw conclusions	separate, estimate, organize, distinguish, appraise, question, prioritize, deduce, integrate, explain, conclude, reason, solve, detect, discover, correlate, focus, support with evidence, interrogate, parse
Evaluating	through checking and critiquing, make judgements and offer opinions based on guidelines, standards, and criteria, and defend your position in the face of opposition	assess, appraise, argue, criticize, judge, decide, defend, critique, comment, test, consider, debate, predict, reflect, check, evaluate, reframe, validate, confirm, determine, hypothesize, speculate
Creating (synthesis)	arising from analysis, put information or knowledge together in an innovative way; reorganize elements into new patterns or structures; generate new ideas and ways of viewing things	synthesize, solve, structure, write, build, integrate, devise, develop, design, plan, create, produce, direct, theorize, invent, manage, predict, construct, devise

(Table continued on next page)

Table 3.4 (Continued)

Bloom's Taxonomy of Learning with Associated Verbs

Learning Domain and Respective Levels of Learning		Associated Verbs
Affective: pertains to the emotional part of learning: attitudes, appreciations, values, interests, opinions, emotions, beliefs, perspectives (five levels)		
Receiving	aware of and willingly attending to certain ideas, stimuli, and phenomena (e.g., just listening or watching)	observe, accept, ask, choose, describe, name, follow, locate, indicate, select, identify, listen, attend to
Responding	actively attending to or reacting to ideas, stimuli, or phenomena with a low level of commitment (e.g., interested— more than just listening or watching)	answer, comply, conform, recite, try, discuss, practice, perform, select, participate, engage in, communicate
Valuing	begin to see things as personally valuable; voluntarily behave according to one's beliefs or attitudes; show preference for an idea or belief by exhibiting an underlying commitment to it	demonstrate, query, follow, form, explain, initiate, describe commitment, propose, justify, support, endorse, monitor
Organizing	organize one's values according to one's priority and integrate into one's existing value system while resolving inner conflicts as they arise; leads to revamped value system prompting self-judgments about one's responsibility to others	prioritize, recognize, adhere to, arrange, defend, explain, order, synthesize, organize, modify, generalize, integrate, recommend, consider, weigh, consult
Characterizing	always behave according to new, internalized value system; integrate this system into a world view or personal philosophy—becomes part of one's *character*	act, discriminate, display, demonstrate, perform, use, verify, practice, profess, commit to, change, criticize, resolve, promulgate, persevere, empathize
Psychomotor: quantity, quality, sequence, and coordination of physical tasks—physical movement, perception, and interpretation (five levels)		
Imitation	repeat or pattern a skill or physical behavior after seeing someone else do it—follow as a model	mimic, copy, follow, replicate, repeat, reproduce, trace, simulate
Manipulation	perform a skill with dexterity by using instructions rather than just imitation or observation; may be a combination of memory and instruction	perform, execute, act, carry out, follow instructions

(Table continued on next page)

Table 3.4 (Continued)

Bloom's Taxonomy of Learning with Associated Verbs

Learning Domain and Respective Levels of Learning		Associated Verbs
Psychomotor: quantity, quality, sequence, and coordination of physical tasks—physical movement, perception, and interpretation (five levels)		
Precision	accurately reproduce and refine a skill with higher degrees of precision (exactness) independent of the original source of material or observation (i.e., no longer need instructions or an external model to mimic, copy, or follow)	demonstrate, master, perfect, calibrate
Articulation	combine (*join*) several well-developed skills in a sequence with consistency and harmony; fluently and smoothly use (articulate) skills to meet special requirements or situations	adapt, adjust, construct, combine, create, alter, customize, modify, formulate, rearrange, vary, revise
Naturalization	complete one or more skills with ease at a high level of performance—it's automatic now with little effort (mental or physical)—second *nature*	design, invent, teach, develop, manage, compose, originate, create

Additional Learning Domains and Perceptions

PSTs and novice teachers are also encouraged to use three additional domains of learning or perceiving that are not included in Bloom's seminal approach—the 3Ps: perceptual, participatory, and proprioception (Diaz et al., 1999; Goble et al., 2009; Hitch & Youatt, 1995; Hooker, 1981).

Perceptual Learning Domain

Perceive is Latin *percipere*, "seize and understand" (Harper, 2022). During perception, information enters the brain along one or more of five sensory *channels*: hearing, seeing, smelling, touching, and tasting. These channels are "perceptual modes" (Frey, 1989, p. 15). Modes are how information itself is *carried* or transferred. Eyes carry an image of fire. Hands carry the heat of fire. The nose carries the smell of smoke. Through these sensory modes (channels), people extract information from their near environment and thereby *perceive* the fire—become aware or conscious of it. What each person <u>does</u> with this *information* (awareness, consciousness) is up to them. The same goes for learners (Frey, 1989).

To appreciate this aspect of learning (aside from the cognitive, affective, and psychomotor domains), Hooker (1980, 1981) conceived the *perpetual* domain of learning with four levels (see Table 3.5). In short, "these levels move *from* perceiving detail *through* classifying forms or patterns, *and* interpreting significance of series of events, *to* insightful decisions and creativity" (Flex, 1989, p. 16, emphases added). Like Bloom's domains of learning, the perceptual domain is hierarchal and cumulative. People move through higher levels of perception as they extract information from the channels bringing it to their brain, and they process it (i.e., seize and understand it). This ascension is possible because teachers can assume that students gain and then hone perceptual abilities at the lower levels to the point that they can change their behavior using what they have learned (called *perceptive performance*) (Hooker, 1980, 1981).

Table 3.5

Perceptual Domain of Learning

Perceptual Domain of Learning Levels	Associated Verbs
Level 1—Sensation (general awareness or impression of something): demonstrate awareness of the informational aspects of stimuli—receive information from as many senses (modes) as feasible and relevant to the learning context	detect, feel, identify, recognize changes, specify degree of change, determine, discriminate, resolve
Level 2—Interpret stimuli into useable information (two perceptual dimensions):	
Figure perception: isolate the object or stimuli from everything else around it, which involves picking things out from an assortment of things in a variety of positions, quantities, qualities, and directions	discriminate, resolve, determine, judge, distinguish, arrange, identify
Symbol perception (symbols are graphic forms such as letters, numbers, punctuation marks, mathematical signs): demonstrate an ability to recognize, name, and rearrange perceived symbols into new patterns or forms	name, distinguish things from each other, read, sort, respond appropriately, rank, indicate, rate, suggest, classify
Level 3—Perception of meaning: (a) interpret stimuli in the larger scheme of things (i.e., explain their meaning, significance, and importance) or (b) assign personal significance to them (what they mean to you)	interpret, determine by action, match, identify cause and effect relationships, judge appropriateness or relevance, attach significance, generalize
Level 4—Perceptive performance: use the processed information and change ongoing behavior by making (a) sensitive, accurate observations and (b) complex, insightful decisions. This higher academic performance is possible due to heightened levels of perception—perceptual learning	sensitive observations, change behavior, analyze, develop plan of action, create, diagnose, demonstrate insight, demonstrate artistry

Source: Hooker (1980, 1981).

Participatory Domain of Learning

Participate is Latin *participare*, "to share in" (Harper, 2022). This domain of learning is especially germane to education that is focused on peace, social justice, global education, citizenship, sustainability, environmental, and/or climate change, wherein teachers want students to become change agents and active participants in their world. In effect, the participatory domain involves helping learners share in their world by (a) understanding global issues themselves and from others' perspectives, (b) developing empathy for others and (c) engaging in activities that develop a sense of self-efficacy. Empathy refers to the arousal of emotions after learning of someone else's circumstance (often inequality, injustice, oppression, marginalization, exploitation). With empathy, students can identity *with* the other person's emotions and respond appropriately with respect and dignity. Self-efficacy is the belief that one is capable of executing a course of action required to manage or change a situation (i.e., "I can *do* this!") (Diaz et al., 1999).

The intent of the participatory domain of learning is thus to help students gain (a) an eye-opening and paradigm-shifting sense of how the world *really* works; (b) how others feel living in that world; and (c) the confidence that they, the student, can change that world. To that end, Diaz et al. (1999) developed a roster of skills required to be a change agent with relevant verbs for the participatory domain of learning (e.g., observe, organize, mobilize, analyze, and strategize) (see Table 3.6).

Table 3.6

Participatory Domain of Learning With Attendant Verbs

- observation
- policy analysis
- research (methods, analysis, and report writing skills)
- take and articulate a position on an issue (advocate and lobby)
- propose actions
- support and justify position taken and actions proposed (critical thinking, logical reasoning, argumentation)
- strategize and network (choose who to approach about the issue and how)
- mobilize support for your proposal (e.g., lead, recruit, manage, coordinate, plan)
- organize actions so change can happen
- deal with resistance by knowing your supporters and opponents
- bargain and negotiate in such a way as to not compromise your cause
- make sure people actually deal with your issue and proposal by getting it on the table, to a vote or get new rules made
- reflect on and evaluate success

Source: Diaz et al. (1999).

Beyond the scope of this primer, appropriate pedagogical instructional strategies would comprise student-centered, authentic learning, which includes problem-based learning; project-based learning; inquiry-based learning; problem posing, naming (problematization), and solving; issues-based learning (especially sensitive and controversial issues); and the use of integrated, theme-based curricula. PSTs and novice teachers would especially try to teach critical and creative thinking, logic and argumentation, strategic planning, advocacy, issues management, leadership and management principles, and self-reflection.

Proprioceptive Processing

The prefix *proprio* means one's own (Anderson, 2014). *Proprioceptive processing* thus refers to someone processing information about their perception of their own body position (i.e., where and how their body parts are moving). Input received through skin, muscles, and joint receptors provides information about one's body placement in relation to other body parts and space (extrabody)—without looking. Proprioceptive processing is also the ability to control the amount of force exerted for different tasks when using different parts of the body. Good examples are holding an egg without breaking it, hugging without hurting, and petting a dog without hitting it (Goble et al., 2009; National Health Services Greater Glasgow and Clyde, 2015).

This aspect of learning should matter to PSTs and novice teachers because it can manifest in academic, social, and behavioral issues in the learning environment masking students' actual ability to learn *if* this condition was acknowledged and accommodated. Students experiencing challenges with this aspect of information processing (e.g., motor control and behavior regulation) can inadvertently engage in, what can be construed as, disruptive behavior (e.g., clumsiness, incoordination, slumping at desk, playing too rough, and banging feet while sitting) (Brain Balance Achievement Center, 2021; Goble et al., 2009). Awareness of its compromised presence can help PSTs and novice teachers properly diagnose the presenting behavior to better help students learn with the use of special, differentiated attention per learning styles (i.e., student accommodation via differentiated instruction—see upcoming section on *Preparing Lesson Plans*).

Learning Goals Versus Learning Objectives

A key part of planning *before* the actual lesson is implemented is identifying learning goals and learning objectives, which teachers develop to reflect various learning domains (see Tables 3.4, 3.5, and 3.6).

Learning Goals

Goals (end point) are where the students should be after completing a large unit of learning (e.g., curriculum, course, module, or unit). Goals are long-term, broad in scope, and general in their intentions but difficult to validate because they are abstract (intangible ideas) rather than concrete (tangible things known through the senses). From a practical standpoint, goal statements "give little assistance to the instructor in a specific class" (Bartel, 1976, p. 113). Instead, goals are a means of communication between curriculum planners and teachers or teachers and parents but not normally with students. Goals are general outcomes that provide overall guidelines but no specific instructional strategies, which is the role of learning *objectives* (Bartel, 1976) (see Table 3.7).

Table 3.7

Examples of Learning Goals in a Global Citizenship Course

The learning goals of this course about global citizenship are for students to
<ul><li>become productive citizens;</li><li>develop an understanding of government and citizen relations;</li><li>develop attitudes of cooperation and consideration with fellow citizens;</li><li>gain richer understandings of global injustice and inequalities manifested through consumption;</li><li>gain deeper insights into the power of ideologies and paradigms; and</li><li>grasp the power wielded by transnational corporations, complicit governments, and ignorant consumers.</li></ul>

Learning Objectives

Objectives are the short- and medium-term, measurable steps and tasks undertaken by the teacher and students to reach learning goals. Objectives are narrow, concrete, and precise. Their attainment can be measured and validated (Kumar, 2011; North American Electric Reliability Corporation [NAERC], 2007). Objectives "serve the function of describing, rather precisely, what the content will be, what responsibilities students and instructors have, and the nature of the evaluation process" (Bartel, 1976, p. 114). For example, the broad goal may be *to know* about the human body. The narrower objectives may include (a) *to* correctly *name* body parts and (b) *to* clearly *explain* how the parts of the body work together as a whole.

PSTs and novice teachers must often teach government-mandated (a) general curriculum outcomes (GCOs) that are equivalent to learning goals and (b) specific curriculum outcomes (SCOs) that are equivalent to learning objectives. GCOs and SCOs are often communicated via subject-matter learning outcome documents published by the Department of Education within state, provincial, territorial, or national governments. Discussing the gambit of these documents is beyond the scope of a primer with the next section focused instead on how to write learning objectives from scratch.

Writing Effective Learning Objectives

Put simply, a learning objective "is a statement describing a proposed [behavioral] change as a result of learning" (Cross, 1973, p. 23). A learning objective clarifies what students are supposed to know—what the teacher intended them to learn. From these objectives, teachers can infer the best instructional strategies to make sure this particular learning happens (NAERC, 2007).

To that end, a learning objective must be as clear as possible, measurable, and workable, and fluent (i.e., students can make sense of it) (Schuman as cited in Schieman et al., 1992). Objectives should also be realistic (within students' abilities), deemed worthy of achieving, and consistent with what has been, is being, or will be taught (Bartel, 1976). A well-written and thought-out objective has four parts: (a) the audience (e.g., the student), (b) the behavior (Bloom's action verb), (c) the conditions and (d) the criteria against which the behavior will be judged (see Figure 3.2).

Figure 3.2

Examples of Learning Objectives

Cognitive (application level) learning objective:

Given a data set, political science students will be able to correctly calculate the government's state of readiness to conduct the 2025 census.

Audience: political science students

Behavior (verb): to calculate government's state of readiness

Conditions: given a set of data

Criteria: correctly, for a particular year (2025)

Psychomotor (manipulation level) learning objective:

Without the use of a spotter, gymnastic students training for the nationals will be able to perform a complete cartwheel in the gym without their hands touching the mat.

Audience: gymnastic students training for nationals

Behavior (verb): to perform a complete cartwheel

Conditions: without a spotter

Criteria: on a mat in the gym; hands cannot touch the mat

Behavior

The behavioral aspect of a learning objective pertains to *what* students will see, think, do, feel, or sense at the end of the instruction. This *what* is indicated using an action *verb* (see previous section on domains of learning and Table 3.4 for examples). Behavioral educational theorists encourage teachers to create *behavioral learning objectives,* but avoid those that are hard to measure, especially ideals and generalizations. To that end, teachers are advised against using such verbs as to appreciate, grasp, respect, prefer, understand, value, or gain insight. By using these verbs, teachers, in effect, have to infer students' learning instead of actually observing and measuring their *behavior* (Bartel, 1976; Fleck 1980; Rao, 2020).

In contrast, advocates of *humanistic learning objectives* favor and value "the development of intelligent behavior *and* [emphasis added] the production of self-directed, creative, problem-solving, humane, and caring citizens who can deal with and contribute to the betterment of our complex society" (Fleck, 1980, p. 265, see also Bartel, 1976). Humanistic learning objectives can include such verbs as to appreciate, respect, and value. These objectives focus on intellectual and emotional processes rather than concrete behavior measured by behavioral objectives (Fleck, 1980). But because students should learn both processes and behaviors, PSTs are encouraged to use both types of objectives.

Educators favoring behavioral objectives agree that the intended learning behavior has to be measurable so teachers can tell whether or not students have learned what was intended. Behavioral objectives refer to "the overt behavior of a student" (Bartel, 1976, p. 117) with overt meaning their *actions* are shown openly and are available for assessment. Teachers indicate the desired action by using an action verb that is prefaced with the infinitive marker *to* and is stated as an infinitive phrase (i.e., the verb lacks a suffix—no *ed, ly, s, tion* or *ing*). Examples include *to* explain, *to* value, *to* demonstrate (McGregor, 2018). There is normally one verb and one idea per learning objective (see Figure 3.2). An objective that is too broad or vague lacks direction and can thus be interpreted in too many ways making it nonachievable or nonmeasurable (Fleck, 1980).

The verb in the learning objective must be consistent with the learning goal. If the goal is *to recall*, the objective should not be about synthesis (e.g., *to integrate*). The same principle holds for the domain of learning. A cognitive domain goal (e.g., to *evaluate*) should not have a psychomotor domain verb (e.g., to *manipulate*). Misalignment risks students not learning what was intended. Finally, PSTs may want to use verbs indicative of higher order learning when writing course, module, or unit objectives and lower order verbs for specific lessons (Cross, 1973; Fleck, 1980; Hitch & Youatt, 1995; Mayer, 1962; NAERC, 2007) (see Table 3.4).

Conditions

Condition is Latin *condicere*, "agree upon" (Harper, 2022). Conditions are the circumstances that affect something's functioning or existence (Anderson, 2014). In a learning objective, the condition is usually a *declarative statement* at the beginning of the objective. This means it makes a declaration (i.e., strives to make things clear)—it makes a statement, provides a fact, offers an explanation, or conveys information. When PSTs and novice teachers prepare learning objectives, they literally impose conditions on the performance (i.e., requirements that must be met to succeed). Conditions set out the context within which the behavior will be performed or demonstrated and can include information, commands, materials, equipment, and any directions that students will receive from the teacher (Bartel, 1976; Mayer, 1962; NAERC, 2007).

Also, conditions can avail *or* deny students access to things and stipulate the setting (parameters, circumstances) for performing the behavior. (a) Teachers can aid the student by making things available to assist their performance (e.g., *Given a* ... mannequin, diagram, set of data, set of guidelines; *Following the* completion of ...; *Using the* recipe provided by the teacher ...). (b) Conditions can also be limiting in that teachers advise students of the parameters within which they are expected to act to demonstrate what they have learned (e.g., *Without the aid* of a diagram, a calculator, a cheat sheet...) (Bartel, 1976; Mayer, 1962; NAERC, 2007).

Criteria

Criteria is Greek *kriterion*, "means of judging" (Harper, 2022). As the word implies, "the criteria part of the objective describes how well the behaviour must be performed to satisfy the intent of the behavioral verb" (NAERC, 2007, p. 2). Against what will the behavior be judged? The criteria indicate the level of mastery or proficiency (psychomotor or cognitive), the depth of thinking (cognitive), or the scope of emotions (affective) (the three learning domains). It is *how well* the student must be able to do the activity—against what standard? What will be accepted as evidence that the student has successfully reached the desired level of intended academic performance? Criteria can include time, tolerance limits, percentages, frequencies, outside standards, permissible errors, degree of excellence, or some combination of these with good reason. At the least, the minimal standard or level of performance acceptable for proof of learning should be indicated (Bartel, 1976; Cross, 1973).

To wrap up, Table 3.8 differentiates among program *goals*, specific program *objectives*, and instructional (behavioral) *learning objectives* and distinguishes among the roles of the overall program, the teacher, and the students (verbatim source: Center for Vocational Education, 1980, p. 9).

Table 3.8

Example of Goals and Objectives

Context	Definition	Example
Program Goals	These include broad statements of **intent** describing what is to be achieved in a (1) total school program, (2) total vocational program, (3) vocational service area, or (4) [an] occupational program within a service area.	To prepare student for entry-level competency in the field of cosmetology.
Specific Program Objectives	These include statements describing the means by which the program goals are to be accomplished, focusing on **teacher** responsibilities as they involve or affect students.	By completion of the program, provide students with technical competency in the field of cosmetology such that they are able to pass the state licensing examination.
Instructional Objectives	These include course, unit, and lesson objectives [that] describe what the **student** is expected to know, accomplish, or be able to do after completing the course, unit, or lesson. Unit and lesson objectives specify (1) the task that is to be preformed, (2) the conditions under which it is to occur, and (3) the acceptable standards of performance.	Given a situation describing the job requirements and opportunities for a position in cosmetology, the student will be able to write and produce a formal letter of application which meets all the criteria as given in the unit checklist.

Source: Center for Vocational Education (1980).

PREPARING LESSON PLANS

Beyond knowledge of learning styles and writing learning objectives, to ensure student learning and effective teaching, PSTs and novice teachers must know how to prepare very detailed lesson plans. A plan is a proposal for how to go about doing or achieving something; a formulated scheme to attain an end (Anderson, 2014; Harper, 2022). Without a written plan, it is harder for teachers to stay on task, on topic, on time, and make on-the-fly adjustments (Hitch & Youatt, 1995).

In that spirit, the lesson *plan* is a guide (i.e., a general direction) rather than written in stone (Fleck, 1980). Teachers must be flexible and intuitive enough to shift gears if warranted while respecting the general intent of the *plan* for the lesson. "The alert teacher will keep tuned in to [students'] new interests and problems and will weave in [students'] ideas and suggestions as the lesson evolves, and will take advantage, too, of [their] own second thoughts" (Fleck, 1980, p. 274). Preparing lesson plans is a skill set that improves with practice and reflective insight, so PSTs and novice teachers must cultivate patience and persistence for this skill set (Alexander & Holland, 2020).

Lesson Plan Development Model

The lesson plan development model herein augments the general approach Fleck (1980) proposed: (a) objectives; (b) supportive learnings (i.e., the actual content to be taught in the lesson and how); (c) pupil experiences (i.e., in-class practice and homework); (d) evaluation; and (e) critical suggestions (adapt the lesson to needs, interests, abilities, and learner types and challenges—in other words, differentiated instruction). The planning model herein is further organized using the *before, during,* and *after* class approach with *class* referring to real and/or virtual meeting time with learners (e.g., classroom, laboratory, field trip, and online platforms).

And the model herein is a modification of Madeline Hunter's seminal approach to lesson planning (M. C. Hunter, 1983, 1984; R. Hunter, 2004). Despite some resistance to her ideas (Johnson, 2000; Wilson, 2021), educational researchers have proven its validity (Stallings, 1985, 1987) and its staying power (Adams & Ray, 2016). Her lesson planning "elements ... have stood the test of time—still used today in many teacher colleges" ("The Madeline Hunter," ca. 1994, p. 1). As recently as 2018, LaMalfa drew heavily on Hunter's approach to develop an instructional design framework for learning. For nearly 20 years, Teachnology (2003) has continued to post at its website Hunter-informed steps for writing a lesson plan.

Table 3.9 (lesson plan development model) is basically self-explanatory and should be read in its entirety. It contains information already covered in this primer (learning goals and learning objectives), new information for this chapter, and steps addressed in upcoming Chapter 5 (assessment and evaluation) (see also Alber, 2012; Lewis, 2019). Using this model, PSTs and novice teachers should be able to avoid the pitfalls of developing mediocre lesson plans. They will be better prepared to (a) engage in good planning that can be shared with authority figures and parents/guardians; and (b) include as many lesson delivery elements as possible to ensure that students are motivated to learn, have a chance to learn, experience teaching that resonates with their learning style and preferences, and can be fairly evaluated on their academic progress and success (Barnett, 2002; Brown, 1994).

As a caveat, the approach in Table 3.9 is conducive to the top-down implementation approach to education and reflects educational philosophies that exclude or minimize students' voices in the learning environment. But it is given weight in this chapter because of the prevailing outcome-based education (OBE) environment premised on predetermined learning outcomes and standards (Rao, 2020). Those authoring an enactment curriculum would be more inclined to use *learning contracts* instead of *lesson plans* (see Anderson et al., 2013). Learning contracts are voluntarily completed by students and signed by them, the instructor and, if relevant, parents or guardians. These documents specify actions the learner promises to take or complete to achieve academic success in the course (Frank & Scharff, 2013).

Table 3.9

Lesson Plan Development Model

Teacher's Name: _____   **Grade Level:** _____   **Name of Course:** _____   **Module or Unit:** _____   **Lesson Title:** _____
PREPARATION **BEFORE** CLASS
LEARNING GOALS: can come from the course outline or the Department of Education's outcome document; Where do you want students to end up? What do you want them to see, think, feel, do, or sense at the end of the lesson?
LEARNING OBJECTIVES for the lesson: measurable steps taken to achieve specific course, module, or unit learning goals; pay attention to action *verbs*, prefaced with *to*, and their proper alignment with the learning goals.
LESSON RATIONALE: *reasons* why students must learn the content/processes in this lesson.
MATERIAL AND EQUIPMENT to be used for this lesson: includes but is not limited to PowerPoints, handouts, flip charts, manipulatives (e.g., tiles, cubes, blocks), work sheets, computers, tablets, other technologies, laboratory setting, pens, pencils, erasers, markers, scissors, rulers, glue, tape, paper clips, whiteout, Bristol board, chalkboard, white board, videos, films, pictures, games, safety procedures.
CONTENT to **be taught** (covered) during the class (approximately 1–3 single-spaced pages of typed text): includes important facts, key concepts, principles, new skills and processes, vocabulary; the amount of content delivered must be a balance between too little and too much for the length of lesson; content must be age-, grade- and learning-style appropriate; must help students achieve lesson's learning objectives.
INSTRUCTIONAL STRATEGIES: planned strategies to teach or deliver the lesson that include but are not limited to lecture, demonstration, modelling, explanations, field trip, guided discussion, handouts, work sheets, break-out groups, independent study, guest speaker, group work, learning stations, laboratory experience, debate, study circle, role playing, games, simulations, projects, films, videos, podcasts, internet research, community service, questioning strategies, self-reflection.

(Table continued on next page)

Table 3.9 (Continued)

Lesson Plan Development Model

TIME: indicate length of lesson and rough estimate of *time* for *each* component of lesson (see below); these time estimates help with the pace; must allot enough time for intended learning (set out in rationale and learning goals).
DURING ACTUAL CLASS
SET: catchy and provocative hook (prompt) to *get, grab,* or *focus* their attention and interest and make them *want* to pay attention to the lesson (about 1–3 minutes). Use mystery, fun, excitement, facts, visuals, senses, and keep it real (e.g., cartoon, ask a question, write saying on the board, video clip, props, do something unexpected).
PACE: things *you will do* to move things along (keep things on track, on topic, *and* on time) so you can pace (control the rate of activity) the delivery of the intended content <u>and</u> the development of *their* learning. Use a timer, have very clear goals for the lesson, have everything prepared, choose most effective way to teach particular content, dovetail, check for understanding, and handle disciplinary issues. These strategies contribute to *the flow* of the lesson—the steady and continuous forward movement.
PRACTICE: activities or learning exercises (if any) that students will do <u>during</u> class time under teacher's supervision to perform or engage with the new learning and gain or improve proficiency and competency (see instructional strategies above).
CHECK FOR UNDERSTANDING: things **you** will do to monitor their progress as lesson progresses. Are they *getting it*? Reply heavily on questioning strategies (see Chapter 4).
CLOSURE: actions, words, or steps **you** take to wrap up the lesson and help students make sense of what was being taught; review and clarify key points of the lesson—main *takeaways* for students. Good closure minimizes confusion and frustration and maintains students' motivation to learn the content.
INDEPENDENT (REINFORCEMENT) PRACTICE both inside (e.g., group, independent, or project work) and outside of class, if any (e.g., homework) without your direct guidance or supervision.
STUDENT ACCOMMODATION: special needs assistance and differentiated instruction, if any.
CURRICULAR CONNECTIONS to previous lessons or other curricula, if appropriate; helps students link lesson content to other subjects they are taking (better chance of learning it).
AFTER CLASS
ASSESSMENT AND EVALUATION: can be performed before, during, or after delivering the lesson (e.g., tests, assignments, student reflections) (see Chapter 5) to gauge how well students learned the content and achieved the learning objectives.
TEACHER'S SELF-REFLECTION on *your own* learning during <u>this</u> lesson-planning process; how do you feel, and what did you learn, about planning, delivering, and evaluating <u>this</u> particular lesson and its contents?

The following narrative teases out four elements that are either not self-explanatory or have nominal information in Table 3.9: lesson rationale, student accommodation, curricular connections, and teacher's personal self-reflection on each lesson.

Lesson Rationale

The lesson rationale explains *why* students must learn what is in the lesson. This set of reasons can be used to explain and justify to others what is being taught or not (e.g., principals, other teachers, parents/guardians, or stakeholders trying to influence the curriculum) (Brown, 1994). "Teachers must make decision about what they will teach and how they will then teach it, decisions that will achieve their purposes and address their students' needs. The value of developing a rationale is that it provides a framework for this planning" (Brown, 1994, p. 1).

Rationales provide the *why* behind choices to focus (or not) on something in a lesson. These statements often contain a purpose (reason) and explanations of why this particular choice is significant. PSTs and novice teachers may have to justify reasons for choosing a particular theory, concept, perspective, resource, activity, or content (subject matter and material). Regardless, rationales often address a gap or a need to be filled (University of Melbourne, 2021). Using the rationale, PSTs and novice teachers can also (a) create a brief agenda of what will be taught in a particular class and why and write it on the board or in a PowerPoint slide, (b) keep students' learning on track (i.e., avoid tangents—cover topics *for* a reason), and (c) create meaningful arrangements within the learning environment (Milkova, 2020).

Student Accommodation

Sometimes *differentiated instruction* is required to address particular students' needs and abilities (Teachnology, 2003); this involves using *different* approaches for different students. This aspect of teacher education is usually covered in courses other than methods courses, hence the truncated version presented in this primer. What follows sensitizes PSTs to the complex topic of differentiating their instruction. Instead of a one-size-fits-all approach, PSTs and novice teachers should try to strategically use instructional and assessment tools that are challenging but fair and that engage all students in meaningful and affirming ways. The ideal result is an *inclusive* learning environment that allows all students to strive for academic success and thrive as learners (EduGains, 2016; Tomlinson, 1999).

In brief, students can vary along many dimensions: learning style and learning preferences; abilities (e.g., psychological, mental, physical, intellectual, and social); sex and gender; socioeconomic status; motivation; language; religion or faith; culture; ethnicity; interests; and more (Ministry of Education, 2007; Tomlinson, 1999). Differentiating instruction is a process teachers employ to make sure that what students learn, how they learn it and how they demonstrate what they have learned "is a match for that student's readiness level, interests, and preferred mode of learning" (Tomlinson, 2004, p. 188).

PSTs and novice teachers can differentiate in four ways. They can change some combination of the (a) learning environment, (b) content taught, (c) processes used to teach and (d) products that students create with attendant expectations of evidence of academic achievement (Ministry of Education, 2007; Tomlinson, 1999). Novice teachers are encouraged to engage in PD and in-service that teaches differentiated, personalized instruction and student accommodation.

As a caveat, a common differentiation approach beyond the scope of this primer is *Individual Program Plans* (IPPs). These are created for learners "who cannot meet the curriculum outcomes of the public-school program, or for whom the outcomes do not apply. The IPP replaces some or all of the outcomes from the public-school program with individualized outcomes" (Nova Scotia Department of Education, 2016, p. 3). Most university BED programs teach PSTs about IPPs. Akin to differentiation, most BED programs orient PSTs to the cultural diversity of today's schools and the significance of culturally relevant curricula and teaching practice. This important topic is beyond the scope of this technical primer.

Curricular Connections

McClain et al. (2000) recommended including curricular and interdisciplinary connections to the topic of the lesson plan. This could entail linking the content to state content standards, other courses being taught in the school, previous courses taken by the students, or even other content in the same course. To illustrate, a lesson about tragic heros in literature could be linked to civics education, global history, journalism, media studies, or theatre and arts curricula (McClain et al., 2000).

Making these connections can help students perceive that what they are learning *is* authentic (real) and relevant to their lives, and it can make other subjects more meaningful. Students gain a more holistic and integrated respect for their entire school curricula instead of seeing everything as piece meal and fragmented (Kelly, 2019b). Students are less likely to pushback and ask, *"Why do I have to learn this? When am I ever going to use this? Why aren't I learning something else?"*

Personal Self-Reflection on Each Lesson

Hunter's (1984) lesson plan model, which informed this chapter, did not include teachers' self-reflection on each lesson (see also "The Madeline Hunter," ca. 1994). But, it is important that PSTs and novice teachers step back and ponder what worked, what did not work and why or why not. It is useful to develop a habit of briefly doing this for each lesson. PSTs could journal wherein they enter their thoughts and monitor their professional growth—lesson by lesson. Table 3.10 provides a roster of recommended questions (there are others of course) that can guide PSTs and novice teachers' self-reflections about the planning for and delivery of a particular lesson (El Concilio of San Mateo County, 2021).

Table 3.10

Recommended Self-Reflection Questions to Critique Each Lesson Taught

> ❐ **Introduction (set)**: Did I arouse students' interest in the topic? Were the learning objectives clear to the group? Did the class settle down in a timely manner?
>
> ❐ **Content**: Was it adequate for topic and the time available? Was it well sequenced? Did I need to adjust the level or amount of content material for this lesson?
>
> ❐ **Interest:** Did I maintain and promote students' interest in the topic to keep the lesson flowing? Did I use a variety of examples and instructional and practice activities to keep them interested and hold their attention?
>
> ❐ **Questioning:** Did I plan and use different sorts of questions to help students' learning progress? Did I promote two-way communication between me and the students and among the students?
>
> ❐ **Student notes (check)**: Did I continually develop a clear chalk or whiteboard summary? Did this summary draw on students' contributions? Did it help students to make their own notes?
>
> ❐ **Teaching aids**: Did I use appropriate audio-visual aids to illustrate and emphasize key points? Were they effective? What would I do differently next time?
>
> ❐ **Group contact (discipline)**: Did I have appropriate control over the learning activities, learning participants, and the progress and flow of the class?
>
> ❐ **Pace of progress**: Did the pace (rate of activities) and flow (direction of movement) suit the *average* members of the class? Did I prepare and apply differentiated instruction if merited?
>
> ❐ **Consolidation (closure)**: Did I stress the main points in the final stages of the class? Did these activities enable students to receive feedback on their learning in this class—help them figure out if they *got it?*
>
> ❐ **Learning outcomes (assessment and evaluation)**: Did students achieve the objectives intended for this session? Am I aware of students who will need more help or more challenging materials?

CREATING LEARNING ENVIRONMENTS

In addition to knowing about (a) student learning styles and learning preferences; (b) writing effective, measurable learning objectives; and (c) planning and delivering daily lessons, PSTs and novice teachers must know (d) how to create a learning environment within which to teach. *Environ* means to surround, enclose, or encompass (Harper, 2022). Adding the suffix *ment* changes the verb environ to a noun, a word used to identify something—*an environment*. Technically, an environment is the surroundings or conditions in which a person operates or lives (Anderson, 2014).

A *learning* environment is thus the conditions within which a person learns (Heick, 2018). "The learning environment can be a powerful teaching instrument at the disposal of the teacher, or it can be an undirected and unrecognized influence on the behaviours of both children and teachers" (Martin, 2002, p. 140). Its strong influence on learning suggests that the learning environment should be consciously created and managed, hence its inclusion in this primer.

Traditionally narrowly construed as the physical classroom setting (e.g., seating arrangements, furniture layout, sound, lighting, and temperature), *learning environments* are now understood to be much more complex. In addition to (a) the physical surroundings and architecture, learning environments also include (b) technological arrangements; (c) a learning culture; (d) learners' characteristics, learning styles, and preferences; (e) curricular goals and intended learning outcomes; (f) school and classroom governing structures; (g) learning resources; (h) assessment and evaluation strategies; and (i) teachers' professional competence and educational philosophy (Davidson et al., 2009; Martin, 2002; Movchan, 2018).

A positive learning environment creates an ambience (atmosphere) that is conducive to students' engagement and motivation to learn (Movchan, 2018). Learning environments can be highly effective, " 'intellectually active' places" (Heick, 2018, para. 1). Creating one involves several interconnected factors and strategies. Related details are provided in Table 3.11, which must be read in its entirety (Davidson et al., 2009; Fleck, 1980; Heick, 2018; Martin, 2002; Movchan, 2018). Aside from physical comfort, the learning environment must address students' diverse intellectual (cognitive), social, psychological (affective), and psychomotor needs. Along with ensuring academic achievement and success, the learning environment must further provide support, care, belongingness, positiveness, growth promotion, human development, self-identity, dignity, and engagement (Fleck, 1980).

Table 3.11

Factors and Strategies Impacting Teachers' Creation of Learning Environments

Establish a supportive learning culture
• help students feel connected to a learning community whether in person or online. • make sure students feel like they are contributing to this culture or community. • consider establishing a mentoring program to perpetuate the learning culture.
Respect students' intrinsic psychological needs
• these can include the need for order and security, belonging, personal power, competence, freedom, fun, respect, dignity, friendships. • on another front, know the students—their socioeconomic background, social and cultural capital, and their cognitive abilities and learning predispositions.
Keep things positive
• reinforce praise, appreciation, and freedom to express their opinions, and minimize humiliation, harassment, and teasing. Remember to address the behavior and not the person.
Provide feedback (information in response to something to aid improvement)
• timely and consistent feedback keeps learners involved and makes them feel like they have a purpose. • feedback can affirm learning and keep learning on track. • done in a positive manner, feedback motivates students to keep learning because they gain insights into their strengths and weak areas.
Celebrate success
• recognizing students' learning success (along many factors) creates a sense of achievement and accomplishment that fosters healthy future learning behavior; this recognition can counter the win-lose mindset of a competitive learning atmosphere that celebrates only the highest scoring students.
Ensure learners' safety
• students learn better if they feel safe, secure, supported, welcomed, and respected—in person and online. Safety pertains to physical, mental (psychological), social, and personal and online privacy. • safety can be ensured by maintaining a healthy learning culture, using codes of conduct and by judiciously, consistently, and respectfully employing disciplinary measures when necessary.
Build positive relationships
• create a collaborative, respectful learning culture that fosters affirming communications and strong interactions among students and with the teacher. • the quality of teacher/student relations (social and academic) deeply affects learning especially students' motivation, commitment, satisfaction, and academic achievement.

(Table continued on next page)

Table 3.11 (Continued)

Factors and Strategies Impacting Teachers' Creation of Learning Environments

Connect classroom to parents/guardians and the community   • students do not live in a vacuum. Teach them that what they are learning is relevant to their future (life and career), their real world, and their community (authentic content).   • create a space where parents and guardians can be heard and play a role in their child's education.
Pay attention to pragmatics and logistics   • seating arrangements, furniture design, room temperature, ambient noise, lighting, and temperature profoundly affect students' learning.   • be aware of floor plan layout and the placement of architectural elements (nooks, windows, doors), filing cabinets, bookshelves, bulletin boards, affixed or mobile blackboards and whiteboards, enclosed and open storage areas (e.g., closets or shelving), sockets and plugins, free floor space, and utility services (gas, water, electricity, solar, wind, wood, propane).   • is there ready space for break-out sessions, group work, self-study, independent study?   • plan technological resources and arrangements ahead of time: computers, tablets, laptops, televisions, radios, internet and Wi-Fi connections, bandwidth, video conferencing platforms, devise-charging. stations, LCD projectors, overhead projectors, smart boards, whiteboards, blackboards, cloud servers, laser printers, 3D printers, photocopiers, flip charts, organizational software, communication software and so on.
Be aware of and shape the school climate   • the school climate refers to conditions that have prevailed over a long time contributing to the learning culture. School climate, culture, and its ethos (i.e., characteristic unique spirit) affect the human atmosphere. School climate matters. What is on the school walls and bulletin boards, what happens on the playground, in the hallways and bathrooms, on the school bus, during lunch, or before and after school—these all reflect the *climate* within the school (e.g., tense, calm, bullish, fearful, violent, tolerant, inclusive, receptive, cliquish).
Be philosophically aware   • teachers can better create a positive learning environment if they step back and think about their philosophy of education (teaching and learning) and do so regularly, alone, and with colleagues.   • what is taught in the classroom and how is affected by teachers' values, principles, beliefs, attitudes, predispositions, and perceptions of learners and education and how these relate to society.
Engage in professional development (PD)   • ongoing PD contributes to teachers' professional competence (subject matter, instructional, pedagogical, and philosophical).   • PD activities can affect teaching beliefs, practices, and pedagogical preferences, which in turn shape how teachers create the learning environment and influence the school climate, culture, and ethos.

CHAPTER 4

DURING CLASS

Teaching Strategies, Questioning Strategies, and Classroom Management

PSTs and novice teachers must have a plan for engaging with students *during* the delivery of the lesson, which involves drawing them *into and through* the lesson. This engagement includes (a) using the set, pace, practice, check, and closure approach (see Table 3.9); (b) judiciously choosing and applying instructional strategies; (c) employing effective questioning strategies; and (d) managing the learning environment (also called classroom management and classroom discipline). As a caveat, information in this chapter resonates most closely with the implementation (top-down) curriculum approach that is focused on predetermined curricular goals and learning outcomes, teacher-determined learning objectives, and a teacher-focused pedagogy with creative licence for student-centered learning when feasible, allowed, or teachers are so inclined.

SET, PACE, PRACTICE, CHECK, AND CLOSURE

In addition to using the set, pace, practice, check, and closure approach (see Table 3.9 for details) when *planning* a lesson, PSTs and novice teachers are especially encouraged to use it when actually delivering a lesson. Together, these actions draw students in, keep them engaged, on track and learning, and wrap things up in a timely manner including assessing to what extent they learned what was intended in that particular lesson (Chamberlain & Kelly, 1981; Hitch & Youatt, 1995; Hunter, 2004; Richards & Renandya, 2002).

Learning to Teach: Primer on Teacher Education Methods, pp. 67–87
Copyright © 2024 by Information Age Publishing
www.infoagepub.com

TEACHING (INSTRUCTIONAL) STRATEGIES

Strategy is Greek *strategia*, "the art of being a general; being in command" (Harper, 2022). This etymological root intimates that PSTs and novice teachers must take command of the lesson planning process and choose actions that will ensure students' learning. "Every time a teacher makes a lesson plan, an important step is to select appropriate techniques for implementing this plan" (Fleck, 1980, p. 221). These techniques are called *teaching strategies* or *instructional strategies* because they form part of a plan of action to achieve a goal or specific purpose, in this case, to deliver a lesson.

Many factors affect the choice of teaching strategy, both academic and pragmatic. PSTs and novice teachers should consider if (a) they are confident using the strategy, (b) the strategy is suitable to the particular learning objectives and lesson content, (c) the strategy does not privilege a particular learning domain, (d) it fits students' maturity levels, (e) it accommodates their academic schedules and (f) provisions can be made for differentiated instruction (Fleck, 1980; Posner & Rudnitsky, 2001; Weston & Cranton, 1986).

Other considerations include (g) class size; (h) length of class period; and (i) time of day, which can affect students' energy levels, attention, and retention. Teachers should also consider (j) floor plans and room layout; (k) lighting, room temperature, and such; and (l) available resources, especially computer technology, audio-visual equipment, printing or photocopying, educational assistants (EAs) for differentiated instruction, and school budgets (Fleck, 1980; Posner & Rudnitsky, 2001; Weston & Cranton, 1986).

From another perspective, teaching and instructional strategies "can be defined as the vehicle or technique for instructor-student communication and can be described in at least four categories: (1) instructor-centered, (2) interactive, (3) individualized, and (4) experiential" (Weston & Cranton, 1986, p. 260). Respectively, examples of instructor-centered strategies include lectures, questioning strategies, and demonstrations. Interactive strategies include class discussions, discussion groups, group projects, and peer teaching. Individualized learning entails students working alone at their own pace with the teacher monitoring and providing feedback on their progress. Experiential learning in secondary schools would include laboratory work, service learning, cooperative (coop) placements, internships, role playing, simulations (imitate real life), and games (Fleck, 1980; Posner & Rudnitsky, 2001; Weston & Cranton, 1986).

The effectiveness of teaching and instructional strategies varies along several trajectories. "In different subject areas, at different levels of instruction, and with different instructors, any one method may or may not be effective, and even within one class, individual students will respond in varying ways to the same teaching method" (Weston & Cranton, 1986, p. 260). Table 3.9 contained a roster of nearly 30 teaching (instructional) strategies (see also Weston & Cranton, 1986). PSTs and novice teachers are encouraged to become familiar with the how-to of each one, practice them over time, and remain vigilant that whatever they choose must work best for student engagement and learning. PSTs are urged to not fall back on one or two comfortable strategies but instead place students' interests first and foremost in their lesson planning and delivery (Fleck, 1980; Posner & Rudnitsky, 2001; Weston & Cranton, 1986).

That said, this primer highlights four extremely common teaching strategies that PSTs will be expected to know when they practice teach and novice teachers must know in their early years as they become more nuanced educators: lectures, discussions, projects, and laboratories.

Lectures

Lecture is Latin *lectura*, "to read or deliver formal discourse; to instruct through oral discourse" (i.e., communication) (Harper, 2022). Lecturing is a one-way communication between the PST or novice teacher and students who are passive recipients of information coming from an expert or authority figure. Lectures are especially good for *explaining* things (i.e., providing understanding to others) (Behr, 1988). They are efficient and effective for lower-level cognitive learning (knowledge and comprehension) with some educators asserting that lectures lose their efficacy in other domains of learning (Hitch & Youatt, 1995; Weston & Cranton, 1986).

Behr (1988) contradicted this assertion by teasing out what *explaining* means. "At a higher level, explaining involves the use of generalisations, cause and effect relationships, as well as reasoning leading to conclusions" (p. 189). He maintained there are three types of explanations. *Descriptive* explanations tell students how processes, structures, and procedures operate using a combination of facts, directions, and illustrations. *Interpretative* explanations clarify the central meaning of a word, statement, or conceptualization. "What does *x* mean?" Finally, *reason-giving* explanations identify a relationship and discuss the cause and effect with explanations ranging from definitive to speculative depending on the state of available information or the existing knowledge base about this issue.

Lectures are often used to present some combination of the who, what, when, why, and how of a topic (Fleck, 1980). They are a useful way to share up-to-date information and innovations. Done well, they also help students "organize the information [they] read [before class], and synthesize it with other sources of information" (Hitch & Youatt, 1995, p. 114). Lectures provide a structure for diverse information—a *cognitive (knowledge) map* into which students can continue to insert new information. Lectures are appropriate when (a) everyone must have the same information, (b) everyone must interpret it the same way or (c) time is limited yet students still need the information. Lectures are a very good way for educators to synthesize materials from several sources (i.e., expedite and streamline the process) and to summarize or delineate important material before moving onto the next part of the course (Hitch & Youatt, 1995). A good lecture has

> a *clarity of structure* and an *interesting presentation*.... Clarity of structure involves defining new terms in explicit language, delineating focal statements in logical sequence and with due emphasis, using carefully chosen examples, and providing an appropriate summary. Interesting presentation involves fluency of expression, [and] variation in voice, gesture and use of teaching aids. (Behr, 1988, p. 191)

Students' dissatisfaction with a not-so-good lecture tends to focus on "incoherence, failure to pitch subject matter at an appropriate level, failure to emphasise main points, inaudibility, reading verbatim from notes, speed of delivery too fast to allow for proper note-taking [sic]" (Behr, 1988, p. 191). Other concerns students express include excessive use of Power-Points in general, too many PowerPoint slides with too little time to read them all, insufficient concrete (working) examples, quizzes and homework not matching the lecture content, a bored and disinterested teacher, and no pauses or breaks during the lecture (Berkeley Center for Teaching and Learning [BCTL], 2021).

To prepare an effective lecture, PSTs and novice teachers must create an overview of a topic and then organize and sequence the content in a logical and clear manner defining pertinent terminology and using examples. While doing this, they must attend to the aforementioned student complaints and concerns (BCTL, 2021; Behr, 1988). Ideally, the PST would build in time for students' questions so at least some two-way interaction is possible. As a dry run, PSTs should read the lecture out loud and time themselves before hand, allowing 20 minutes for a 30-minute class. If scaffolding the lecture with PowerPoints, allow at least one minute per slide (Bartsch & Cobern, 2003; Behr, 1988; Fleck, 1980; Weston & Cranton, 1986).

Materials commonly used with the lecture technique include a podium, microphone, handouts (paper or online), PowerPoints, Prezzies or Visme (and other digital tools), overhead projector and transparencies, liquid-crystal display (LCD) projector and computer, chalk and blackboards, markers and whiteboards, erasers, and online learning platforms (Bartsch & Cobern, 2003; Behr, 1988; Fleck, 1980; Weston & Cranton, 1986).

Discussions

Discuss means writing or talking about something in detail to reach insights, a conclusion or a decision (Anderson, 2014; Hitch & Youatt, 1995). PSTs and novice teachers can use both class discussions and group discussions. Respectively, *class discussions* involve the entire class (usually smallish in size <15) conversing together after the teacher has provided an issue, a question, or a topic of interest. Students back and fro with their own points of view and relevant arguments scaffolded with the PST or novice teacher guiding the interchange. This technique is very appropriate for higher levels of the cognitive domain and all levels of the affective domain of learning. Break-out *group discussions* (three to seven per group) are good for instances when (a) the class is very large (>30), (b) students' interests vary or (c) some of the students learn better in small groups (differentiated learning) (Hitch & Youatt, 1995; Weston & Cranton, 1986).

PSTs are cautioned to not assume that *"anyone* can lead a discussion." This skill must be learned through practice. It is more than a conversation (informal exchange) because a discussion leads to some conclusion, insight, or decision (Hitch & Youatt, 1995). Discussion "is a technique whereby a group or class, under the guidance of a leader, examines its views of a problem through group interaction, then attempts to reach the best solution possible" (Fleck, 1980, p. 235). Discussions are not appropriate for every lesson, but they work well with higher level cognitive and affective learning (Weston & Cranton, 1986). They can be used for a variety of reasons: (a) problem solving, (b) sharing diverse points of view, (c) developing motivation, (d) applying principles or (e) developing and expressing logic and assessing an argument's validity (Alexander et al., 2020; Hitch & Youatt, 1995).

The topic of discussion must resonate with students and have significance and meaning for them. The PST or novice teacher's role is to introduce and then guide the discussion (about content-related issues) while balancing the extent of their own involvement (i.e., talk but not take over). PSTs must ensure that all students have the chance to participate and contribute to the discussion. A positive emotional climate has to be created that is safe for dialogue and expressing resistance to each others' ideas. PSTs and novice teachers can provide issue-specific background reading or simply have students draw on learning to date within the course. Other teaching considerations include movability of furniture, length of class period, and acceptable discussant behaviour (e.g., respectful, ethical) (Fleck, 1980; Hitch & Youatt, 1995; Weston & Cranton, 1986).

Pragmatically, PSTs and novice teachers are encouraged to (a) use warm-up exercises to jump start the discussion scaffolded with starter questions, (b) establish small buzz groups to kick start a lagging discussion or (c) pull things together to reach some conclusion or measure some learning objective (Fleck, 1980; Hitch & Youatt, 1995). After all, discuss is Latin *discutere*, "to dash to pieces, to investigate" (Harper, 2022) intimating that learning depends on pulling the pieces back to together after dashing them apart while investigating an issue.

Projects

Project is Latin *projecte*, "a design, scheme, draft, plan" (Harper, 2022). A project is a learning enterprise carefully planned to achieve a particular learning goal or learning objective—the end result reflects content-based material. Some educators distinguish between *doing* a project and project-based learning (PBL). Using a food metaphor, the latter *is* the main course, and the former is the dessert (an assignment within a course) (Buck Institute for Education, n.d.). An in-course project often happens at the end of a unit after the teacher has delivered a traditional lesson using lectures, worksheets, and readings or some combination (Buck Institute for Education, n.d.). Some educators argue that this sort of project approach does not instill deep learning—it is more so the application of principles than critical thinking (see Woodruff, 1961).

Conversely, PBL is driven by students' critical inquiry and discovery and is focused on both the process and the product (not just the final product). It requires sustained inquiry, investigation, thinking, research, writing, and self-reflection (Buck Institute for Education, n.d.). Using the PBL teaching or instructional strategy, the PST or novice teacher sets the learning goals and objectives but enables students to explore the topic and create a project (alone or with others) to provide evidence of their learning. The teacher acts as a facilitator and scaffolds (supports) the learning experience by (a) monitoring students' progress toward learning objectives, (b) providing actual or access to resources, (c) engendering encouragement and support and (d) offering guidance when necessary or solicited. The teacher must ensure that the project is content driven and that students stay on task (Amidon et al., ca. 2018; Weston & Cranston, 1986).

PBL projects either present a (a) phenomenon to investigate or (b) a problem to solve. Respectfully, *"What causes pollution?"* and *"What is the best way to reduce pollution in the town's downtown core?"* To reflect what they have learned and how their knowledge base has advanced, students can (a) prepare a written or oral report or presentation (e.g., term paper, Blog, script for a play, a town hall speech); (b) create a physical product or artifact (e.g., drawings, paintings, videos, photographs, posters, PowerPoints, Prezzi, Sutori, and Pinterest); or (c) create a new or revised service offering (e.g., a new bus route, school recycling program, or mobile community library service). Beyond learning just answers to questions, PBL projects let students expand their mind and think beyond how they normally would because they are not dependent on the teacher but on themselves and other students (Amidon et al., ca. 2018).

Laboratories

Laboratory learning (a form of simulation of real life) gives students the chance to perform and learn protocol and processes in somewhat realistic situations under the PST or novice teacher's careful control (e.g., food, clothing, chemistry, biology, physics, or computer labs). Labs are especially appropriate for learning skills to be applied in real situations, which, for practical, economic, or safety reasons, must instead be learned and practiced in a contrived environment in a school setting. This teaching or instructional strategy is very appropriate for the cognitive and psychomotor domains of learning. Students gain opportunities to (a) learn and apply a skill; (b) learn and apply a principle; and/or (c) experiment firsthand with materials, procedures, processes, protocols, and people (Chamberlain & Kelly, 1981; Fleck, 1980; Hitch & Youatt, 1995; Weston & Cranton, 1986).

An effective laboratory lesson must be well-planned, coordinated, and supervised. Respectively, a *plan* is a detailed outline for doing or achieving something. *Coordination* brings a variety of elements into an efficient arrangement (e.g., students, time, materials, and space). *Supervision* entails observing and directing students' performance to get the lab work done on time and in a way that they learn. The instructor acts as a resource and a guide. Lack of these three traits means the laboratory learning experience may be ineffectual, frustrating, and even dangerous (Anderson, 2014; Chamberlain & Kelly, 1981; Hitch & Youatt, 1995).

To lessen the chances of a negative or unsafe learning experience, during the lab itself, PSTs and novice teachers could ensure that everyone is wearing a name badge but must ensure awareness of time constraints and safety protocols. Teachers should speak to a student instead of yelling across the room. PSTs should give directions only when necessary to minimize affecting the flow and pace of the lab work. Being friendly, firm, and fair is recommended, but negative or careless student behaviour should be addressed if it compromises safety or learning (Chamberlain & Kelly, 1981; Hitch & Youatt, 1995).

Overall, when using the laboratory strategy, PSTs and novice teachers must consider several key factors: (a) carefully plan the work schedule to fit within time constraints; (b) spread the work load by teaching how and appointing students to clean up, replace supplies and equipment, and complete other laboratory tasks; (c) orient students to safety protocols; and

(d) build in time (or expectations) for debriefing and evaluating the laboratory learning experience (generalizations and specifics) (Chamberlain & Kelly, 1981; Fleck, 1980; Hitch & Youatt, 1995).

QUESTIONING STRATEGIES

Teachers pose between 300 and 400 questions a day (McComas & Abraham, 2004). Question is Latin *quaerere*, "to ask or seek" (Harper, 2022). A question is simply a sentence worded (asked) to obtain (seek) information (Anderson, 2014; Cotton, 1988). Questions posed by teachers are "instructional cues or stimuli that convey to students the content elements to be learned" (Cotton, 1988, p. 1). That is, if a teacher asks about something, it must be important. PSTs and novice teachers must know how to develop and ask (pose) good questions and respond to students' answers, so they can assess, affirm, correct, and advance students' learning. "Developing skills in questioning for understanding and content knowledge evolves over time and like anything else, requires practice. The payoff is significant in terms of students' conceptual understanding" (Ontario Ministry of Education, 2011, p. 8; see also Gaetz, 2002; Gross Davis, 1999).

Questioning is frequently used with other instructional methods (Hatch & Youatt, 1995) but is treated separately in this primer because many people erroneously assume that it is easy to do. To aid PSTs and novice teachers in gaining and honing this skill, this section discusses the (a) purpose of questioning, (b) types of questions, (c) ins and outs of developing and asking questions and fielding students' answers and (d) indicators of a successful questioning strategy. A guiding principle underpinning this section is that questioning strategies are important because students' thinking and their academic progress and achievement are not answer driven, but question driven (Gaetz, 2002).

Purpose of Questioning

Overall, the *right* questions (i.e., relevant, and meaningful to the course content) will help students to (a) learn, connect, and apply concepts and principles; (b) think critically and creatively, broadly and deeply; (c) explore logic and understanding at deep levels; (d) extend their thinking by justifying their answers; (e) gain experience with causation, predictions, and hypotheticals; (e) be self-reflective; and (f) think on their own and pursue knowledge on their own. Questions also help teachers determine what students know and do not know, how (if, to what extent) they understand it, and questions help solicit information for teacher's feedback to students

(Afflerbach, 2007; Gaetz, 2002; Gross Davis, 1999; Hitch & Youatt, 1995; McGough & Nyberg, 2015; Sheffield, 2002).

Teachers can use questions to kick-start a lesson, move from one part of the lesson to another, keep students focused and hold their attention, and wrap up the lesson. Through using questions, PSTs and novice teachers can better ensure they achieve the learning objectives, check students' understanding, identify and clarify misunderstandings, and create a community of learners. Questions also help build the learning environment, contribute to the dynamics of the learning climate, and, in some instances, can hold learners accountable for their own learning. Questions can be springboards for discussions, lead students to consider new and different ideas, and stimulate full-group participation (Harrison & Blakemore, 1992; Hitch & Youatt, 1995; McComas & Abraham, 2004; McGough & Nyberg, 2015; Sheffield, 2002). As a caveat, questions are best used as a diagnostic tool to assess students' academic progress rather than as a classroom management technique (Croom, 2004).

Types of Questions

Questions can concern several mental and intellectual processes: recall, interpretation, inference, assumptions, implications, perspectives and points of view, predictions, logic, affect and effect, meaning, and relevance—to name a few (Dantonio, 1990; Erickson, 2007). Table 4.1 profiles a wide range of question types with their explanation and examples (Dantonio, 1990; Erickson, 2007; Mind Tools Content Team, 2013; Peterman, 1998; Wilson, 2021; Wolf, 1987). This inventory of questions is not conclusive, but it is quite inclusive. PSTs and novice teachers are encouraged to read Table 4.1 in its entirety. The *explained* column contains valuable information about the intent of questioning and, by association, the nuances of what constitutes student learning in its myriad forms.

When creating Table 4.1, distinctions were made between question types that (a) are planned ahead of time and those that (b) spontaneously emerge as the lesson unfolds (Afflerbach, 2007). Questions planned ahead of time are more likely to involve students' "thinking, recalling ideas and experiences, weighing ideas against each other, trying out new interpretations of old experiences, and considering evidences [sic] for and against a conclusion" (Woodruff, 1961, pp. 146–147). That said, the question types in Table 4.1 are not mutually exclusive (i.e., some types *can* be prepared ahead of time and created on the fly) (Afflerbach, 2007). Fortunately, "students benefit from a mixture of spontaneous and planned questions" (Afflerbach, 2007, p. 126).

Table 4.1

Types of Questions to Use During Teaching

Question Type	Explained	Example
Planned Before the Class		
Factual/closed	recall specific information, check facts, and uncover misconceptions that can then be challenged and addressed; the answer is either right or wrong; avoid posing these questions if there is good conversation going on because doing so could shut it down	*"What is the name of the Shakespearean play about two teenage lovers?"*
Open	help promote debate and discussion; can be answered in a variety of acceptable ways normally with longer responses than closed questions; require students to explain and defend their answers	*"You are right, but why?" "How else could Shakespeare have dealt with the feud and Romeo and Juliet's love?" "Why do you think Romeo and Juliet reacted the way they did?"*
Convergent	*converge* means come together from different directions to meet; answers are within a finite range of acceptable accuracy or rightness; assumes students' answers will be identical or very similar	*"On reflecting on the entire play of 'Romeo and Juliet,' what were the main reasons for the family feud that put the young lovers in such a deadly predicament?"*
Divergent	*diverge* means to separate from a shared route to go in different directions; there is no right answer; instead, through analysis, synthesis, and evaluation (and imagination, curiosity, and research), students explore possibilities and different avenues and create many variations and alternative answers or scenarios	*"In Shakespeare's play 'Romeo and Juliet,' what might have happened to the teens if the family feud had come to an end?" "What do you suppose would happen if the government passed a law legalizing marijuana?"*
Hypothesis	*hypothesize* means drawing suppositions based on limited evidence; to answer, students must think of new situations; they use what they have learned or been exposed to so far and predict; fosters critical awareness of their expectations	*"Starting from the exchange between the two characters in Chapter 3, what are three or four new things you could add to open up their dialogue?"*
Evaluative	*evaluate* means to form an idea of the significance or worth of something: students draw on higher order cognitive (logical) and affective (emotive) levels of learning or on comparative frameworks. This requires them to analyze, synthesize, and evaluate	*What are the similarities and differences in Juliet and Ophelia's deaths?*

(Table continued on next page)

Table 4.1 (Continued)

Types of Questions to Use During Teaching

Question Type	Explained	Example
Planned Before the Class		
Inference	*infer* means reach a conclusion based on reasoning; students go beyond immediately available information and fill in missing information; they find clues, examine them, and then discuss inferences with justification	*"What do you know by looking at this photograph?"* Possible answers include where, when, and who (both photographer and the subject), technique (lighting, perspective, filters), meaning, messages
Interpretation	what does it *mean* that something is there or not? Students discern the consequences of ideas or information	*"How would this picture and its message be different if the model was not wearing the diamond necklace?" "What do you think the diamond necklace represents or means?"*
Transfer	students take what they know to new places (different from the context where they learned it); expect them to expand their thoughts by provoking breadth (wide range) of thinking	Exam question: *This semester, we studied three film directors. Pretending to be a film critic, write a review of the Disney movie 'Cinderella' as if it were directed by one of these individuals.*
Organizing	*organize* means arrange systematically; students determine sequences, outcomes, consequences, cause and effect, similarities, differences	*"Suppose ... (a specific situation). What do you expect is going to happen?" "How are x and y similar and different and why?" "Please explain why such and such happens?"*
Contextualizing	students appreciate the conditions and context (set of circumstances surrounding something) within which they exist and how this context shapes their understandings; questions asked elicit beliefs, values, attitudes, opinions	*"Under what conditions did slavery happen in United States?" "Upon what values is that situation based?" "Upon what assumptions was slavery based?"*
Spontaneously Asked During the Class		
Probing (elaborate, clarify, extend, verify)	accept or acknowledge students' initial response and then move beyond it – prompt them for more: get them to clarify, think more carefully, be more critical, or express their answer differently	*"Why do you think that?" "What evidence supports your idea?" "Can you elaborate on that point?" "Can you please explain what you mean?" "Can you say that in a different way?"*

(Table continued on next page)

Table 4.1 (Continued)

Types of Questions to Use During Teaching

Question Type	Explained	Example
Spontaneously Asked During the Class		
Focus	delineate what students are trying to figure out (get to the center of things; brings things into sharper focus); help them make complex connections among big ideas; also, focus-type questions can get students to name, describe, and categorize what they know (lists, labels, groups)	*"What can the table of contents and the index tell us about the author?" "What makes a book a book?" "What key parts are used to make a motorcycle?"*
Managerial (structuring)	aids progression through the lesson and keeps the flow of learning moving	*"Are there any questions?" "Is the assignment clear?" "Are we ready to continue?" "Which parts of the lesson did you not understand well?"*
Call out	ask a question of no one in particular— keep these to a bare minimum	*"Who can tell me how many national parks there are in Canada?"*
Hinge	write a multiple-choice question on the black or whiteboard or PPT slide to see if students are ready to move onto the next portion of the lesson or if the teacher needs to reteach or recap the main points; teacher's next step *hinges* on the students' answers	*"Which of the following sentences is an example of alliteration?* *1. The golden disc of the sun burned.* *2. Sunday's sizzling summer sun shone strongly.* *3. I felt the hot red sun on my face.* *4. The sun-dappled leaves moved gently."*
Reflective	students look inward and express assumptions, confusions, major premises, suppositions, hypotheses, speculations	*"Given that answer, what things did you assume rather than examine?" "When you think about...?" "As you consider...?"*
Thought-provoking	students mindfully engage with the course content using their insight and reasoning—these questions cannot be answered simply	*"What have you come to know or now know differently?" "What would have to happen in order for...?"*
Hypothetical	students speculate (i.e., they form a theory or conjecture without firm evidence)	*"What would happen if we did it this way?" "What would happen if we left out this step?"*
Rhetorical	not really a question but a statement in question form that is used to reinforce an idea or emphasize a point; students infer from the teacher's rhetorical statement that the content contained in the idea is important thus they must learn it	*"Isn't Star Trek's script writer really good at drawing on myths and mythology?" "We need iron and protein in our diet, right?"*

Developing and Asking Questions

PSTs and novice teachers need three separate questioning skill sets, including how to (a) develop good questions, (b) ask them and (c) then respond to students' answers. These skills are referred to as "questioning techniques" (Hitch & Youatt, 1995, p. 126) with technique meaning a way of carrying out a particular task (Anderson, 2014). Table 4.2 provides a roster of recommended techniques and guidelines for developing questions ahead of time while creating a lesson plan for the class (Bonwell & Eison, 1991; Cotton, 1988; Dantonio, 1990; Gross Davis, 1999; Hitch & Youatt, 1995; McComas &Abraham, 2004; Ontario Ministry of Education, 2011).

Table 4.2

Techniques and Guidelines for Developing Questions Ahead of Time

- make sure questions relate to the lesson's content.
- questions must be at an appropriate level of materials being covered.
- use vocabulary familiar to students.
- questions must reflect the lesson's learning objectives (see Table 3.3)
- respect different learning styles and learning preferences (see Chapter 3).
- develop questions from all three learning domains in Bloom's taxonomy (*if* relevant to the lesson) and from multiple levels within each domain (again, if relevant to the lesson) (see Table 3.4); in other words, do not privilege the cognitive domain. When relevant, also pose questions from the three non-Bloom learning domains (see Figure 3.1).
- per above, plan higher order questions in advance and limit lower order questions to spontaneous ones as the lesson unfolds.
- draw on the full range of question types (see Table 4.1) relative to what is needed to learn the content, achieve the learning objectives, and gauge students' depth of learning.
- develop questions before and after writing up the lesson plan, and *then* adjust questions accordingly when actually delivering the lesson.
- questions must be clear, concise, and not ambiguous (cannot have more than one meaning and should not cause students to be perplexed or confused).
- the question should contain only one idea.
- focus on most important parts of lesson's content (students take cues about what is important to learn)
- create questions of varying difficulty.
- balance the number of questions intended for the whole class with those intended for individual students.
- ask students to develop their own questions while doing their homework or readings and bring to class.
- prepare and give questions to students in advance; they bring answers back to class to expedite discussion.

"Skilled teachers question in distinct ways: they raise a range of questions, they sustain and build arcs of questions, their inquiries are authentic, they inquire with a sense of respect flail decency" (Wolf, 1987, p. 2). Table 4.3 (must be read in its entirety) showcases a wide-ranging roster of techniques for establishing the question climate, asking questions, and responding to students' answers (Bonwell & Eison, 1991; Cohen, 1978; Dantonio, 1990; Gaetz, 2002; Gross Davis, 1999; Harrison & Blakemore, 1992; McComas & Abraham, 2004; Oklahoma Baptist University [OBU], ca. 2000; Sheffield, 2002; University of Delaware, 2002; University of Waterloo, 2021).

Table 4.3

Techniques and Guidelines for Developing Questions Ahead of Time

Establishing Question Climate

- create a question-friendly, active-learning environment—let students know that they are expected to ask questions too because posing a question represents great progress in their comprehension.

- engage in active listening (i.e., do not think about what you are going to say next—actually listen to the student's words, so you can paraphrase and reflect back what they said if need be).

- also, *listen* to the subtext (look between the lines, body language, who is listening, who is disengaged, who is hesitant).

- use positive body language and nonverbal cues, and avoid a condescending or put-down tone when responding to their answers—this contributes to a positive questioning climate and culture.

Asking (Posing) Questions to Students

- ask the question to the entire class before asking a particular student to answer (this way, everyone thinks).

- per above, allow sufficient time (20–30 seconds) for all students to frame an answer before calling on anyone in particular; doing otherwise allows students to remain passive; *KEY: learn to enjoy the silence.*

- avoid run-on questions and rapid-fire questions; wait at least 10 seconds before posing another question.

- if a student you ask hesitates to answer, tell him or her to think about it and you will come back later.

- give students a chance to pass (two passes per class).

(Table continues on next page)

Table 4.3 (Continued)

Techniques and Guidelines for Developing Questions Ahead of Time

---

Asking (Posing) Questions to Students

- ask already prepared questions in an orderly sequence (an arc of questions) so discerning students can see a purpose to the questions and identify their order and the reasoning behind them.

- introduce question at the appropriate time not just for sake of asking it because it was already prepared.

- per above, adapt previously prepared wording if original wording does not resonate with students.

- call on students randomly (ideally have a class list of names); do not always pick student with their hand up.

- stand closer to students who tend not to answer (closer proximity can elicit a response).

- make sure there is wide participation of students (both volunteers and reluctant or reticent nonvolunteers).

- be very conscious of the wait-time principle (*the pause*); deliberately wait a minimum of 5–10 seconds. (I\ideally 20–30 seconds) after asking a question; learn to enjoy the silence—it means students are thinking.

- if necessary, rephrase the question after the wait time.

- keep wait time to 2–3 seconds for lower order questions and longer for higher order questions (minimum 5–10 seconds).

- avoid "*Does everyone understand?*"; instead add qualifying phrases to modify the original question (limit or enhance it) to guide students to their answers.

- avoid leading questions (e.g., "*Don't you think that...?*") by using neutral language ("*What are your thoughts on ...?*").

- minimize yes/no questions unless needed on the spot to discern retention,

- minimize posing simplistic questions with obvious answers (they are acceptable for getting things rolling).

- minimize answering the question yourself – give students time to think; welcome their silence.

(Table continues on next page)

Table 4.3 (Continued)

Techniques and Guidelines for Developing Questions Ahead of Time

Responding to Students' Answers

- do not interrupt a student's answer (need to know if credit is due or if more learning is required).

- look at students while they answer; use facial expressions and body language to indicate paying attention.

- if answer is off topic, thank student for answering and rephrase the question for the class.

- redirect question to another student after an initial answer ("*Annette, can you add something else?*").

- reinforce correct answers as well as the correct portion of a partially correct answer.

- per above, do not dismiss a student's contribution if their answer is wrong or weak; instead, find something positive to lead the class back to the learning objective.

- if the answer *is* incorrect or weak, ask the student to explain their answer (could be a misunderstanding of the question or insufficient information to answer).

- when students indicate they do not understand the question, do not repeat it—rephrase it or provide cues.

- praise good answers using a variety of responses, but do not praise excessively because unpraised. students may assume their answers are always no good and quit answering.

- answer a student's question with "*What do* you *think?*" directing it either to that person or the whole class.

- turn a student's answer into a chance to hear other students' answers "*Listen to another explanation and then tell me whether it means the same thing as what you just said.*"

- instead of responding to student's answer right away, ask other students to respond to the student's answer.

- find a way to enter into a discussion with student(s) instead of moving onto the next question right away.

- repeat a student's question if the class could not hear it well.

- rephrase a student's long, convoluted question or comment so others can engage with it.

- ask all students to write down their answer and then call on several to read theirs—this way, *all* students have to think and can unobtrusively compare their answer to others and learn.

- ask the other students to answer a student's question then encourage class discussion.

- admit if you do not know the answer "*That's a good question. I'm not sure about that. Let's....*"

- per the above, if you do not know the answer, get students to brainstorm answers thereby creating. excitement for exploring the unknown. Find the answer (or get them to find it) and bring it to the next class.

Discerning Effectiveness of Questioning Strategy

"Questions have always been the backbone of effective teaching. [They] are the heart of knowledge" (Gaetz, 2002, p. 10). Without questions, students have a harder time of gaining new information that can be turned into new knowledge. Preservice and in-service professional development training that sharpens teachers' questioning skills can help educators increase students' academic achievement (Cotton, 1988). Joyce and Showers (1988) called this "student achievement through staff development" (Title). In the meantime, PSTs and novice teachers are encouraged to self-reflect on the success of their questioning strategy to determine if it was effective in the short and long term (McComas & Abraham, 2004; OBU, ca. 2000).

In brief, a questioning strategy is successful *if* (a) the questions sustained the learning process, (b) students remained interested and engaged, (c) learning objectives were achieved and (d) students learned the course content. The questions may have revealed (e) misconceptions and misunderstandings and (f) degrees of learning success among students thus establishing a foundation for additional required learning or readiness for new learning. Ideally, (g) class rapport was bolstered, (h) diverse learners were accommodated and (i) collaborative participation was evident (McComas & Abraham, 2004; OBU, ca. 2000).

CLASSROOM MANAGEMENT

"Classrooms are populated by groups of students assembled under crowded conditions for relatively long periods of time to accomplish specified purposes" (Doyle, 1989, p. 15). Group dynamics and individual student's lives manifest in many ways in these school settings. PSTs and novice teachers must be prepared to handle disruptions to learning, which are to be expected in complex, confined classroom settings. This skill set is often called *classroom management* (Doyle, 1989; Fleck, 1980; Larrivee, 2005) with management meaning (a) being in charge of or controlling something, (b) supervising others' activities, (c) regulating others' behavior and (d) administering justice and discipline via rules and (in)formal codes of conduct (Anderson, 2014).

Fleck (1980) referred to "the management of the learning environment" and framed the "teacher as a manager" (p. 157). PSTs and novice teachers can go about this management task in one of two ways: proactively and reactively (Doyle, 1989; Fleck, 1980). *Proactively*, they can *create* positive relationships with students by treating them with dignity and respect; making them feel needed and that they belong; and involving them in the daily responsibilities inherent in running the learning environment (e.g., help maintain supplies, keep an orderly learning space, create bulletin boards, or act as student aids) (Fleck, 1980).

Reactively, PSTs and novice teachers would respond to situations that disrupt and distract learning. This is often called *disciplining* students with the common assumption that their behaviour merits rebuke or punishment. Interestingly (ironically), discipline is Latin *disciplina*, 'to learn, instruction, knowledge' (Harper, 2022). Fleck (1980) assumed this perspective when she proposed "*suggestions for maintaining discipline*" (p. 163) by which she meant *maintaining learning*. In saged advice, Fleck noted that "students are happier and more productive if they know, understand, and help to establish the regulations governing their [learning] situation. Students gain a sense of security when they learn that consistent rules are important for effective group learning" (pp. 162–163).

As a caveat, Shindler (2010) astutely observed that "the most effective strategies for technical management can be some of the most unnatural and counterintuitive practices one comes across [because] they are not what we do naturally in the world outside school. They are probably not what our common sense tells us to do. However, [they work]" (p. 82). This caveat (and the information that follows) applies to all classrooms (Shindler, 2010). Table 4.4 provides a roster of suggestions that PSTs and novice teachers can turn to as they learn the skill set of managing the learning environment they have created, so that learning can be maintained (Doyle, 1989; Fleck, 1980).

PSTs and novice teachers are further encouraged to "experiment with various techniques. Get ideas from other teachers, from reading, and from observation. Develop some unique measures" (Fleck, 1980, p. 163). Doyle (1989) observed that "successful interventions occur early in response to misbehavior, are often quite brief, and do not invite further comment from the target student or students" (p. 18). This success is more likely if teachers use "a variety of unobtrusive nonverbal signals (e.g., gestures, direct eye contact, and proximity) to regulate [the learning-disruptive behavior]" (Doyle, 1989, p. 18).

Of note is that the traditional, teacher-controlled, and teacher-directed classroom (still the norm) is evolving to a more student-centered approach, which necessitates a different approach to *managing* the classroom (Larrivee, 2005). Examples include both authentic, and transformative classroom management, which are briefly introduced but not elaborated on in this primer.

Table 4.4

Specific Suggestions for Maintaining Discipline (Uninterrupted Learning)

- always be aware of what is happening in the learning environment and learn to attend to several events at the same time (dovetail).
- intentionally monitor pace, flow, rhythm, and duration of various parts of the lesson (any prolonged. delays, or students' perception of teacher not being in control, can trigger disruptive events).
- touch finger to closed lips to stop two students from talking with each other.
- talk low to get the attention of the class (may be more effective than raising voice or yelling).
- silently shake your head to indicate their need to stop the disruptive behavior.
- move to and stand close to them but keep teaching.
- try a timely, humorous remark (but not disparaging, ridiculing, or mocking).
- experiment with *the pause* (stop talking and wait 10 seconds or more until they notice the silence).
- make students feel respected and valued (accept that they are *still learning* self-discipline and self-regulation).
- if possible, modulate (alter or adjust) one's voice so students respond more positively when hearing it.
- critically enforce well-established rules, which must not be vague or open to interpretation.
- manipulate classroom logistics (seating arrangements, lighting, heat, noise, and such).
- deal with a particular student rather than punish the whole class (avoid group punishment).
- minimize holding students after class (this sort of discipline defies the principles of learning).
- accept that each student's behaviour *will* vary (students are maturing and learning self-discipline) but be aware of abrupt shifts in a particular student's patterns of behavior.
- ask students to write their own report of their "misbehavior'" (this way, they get to practice self-discipline).
- keep a record of students struggling with self-discipline (repeatedly causing learning disruptions).
- when all these soft techniques do not work, turn to advice, and seek help from school counsellor or other. experts (psychological, pathological, social, academic) and arrange consults with parents or guardians.
- turn to colleagues as well as school administrators (principal, vice principals, department chairs) for help and support with the student's best interest in mind—always.

Authentic Classroom Management

Some PSTs and novice teachers may embrace a student-centered educational philosophy (see Chapter 1). For them, the classroom management strategies set out in Table 4.4 may feel antithetical to (incompatible with) what is involved in managing an authentic classroom where learning is focused on students with teachers acting as facilitators, guides, and coaches. In these instances, authentic classroom management would be more appropriate wherein (a) teachers are expected to be self-aware, self-reflective practitioners; (b) the learning climate validates and accommodates the diverse needs of all learners; (c) democratic values are respected and modelled; and (d) teachers share power with students instead of exerting authority and power over them (Larrivee, 2005).

When managing this type of learning environment, PSTs and novice teachers would focus on prevention (proactive) rather than intervention (reactive) strategies but employ the latter when necessary for the students' well-being (see Table 4.4). *Prevention* includes (a) creating and building a democratic learning community; (b) keeping the lines of communication open to enhance the flow of authentic, respectful listening and talking; (c) ensuring collaborative and cooperative participation; (d) managing by rewards and consequences instead of punishment; (e) developing self-regulated and self-disciplined students; and (f) respectfully employing conflict and stress management strategies (e.g., rights and responsibilities, assertion not aggression, resolution) (Larrivee, 2005). Beyond the scope of this primer, PSTs and novice teachers are encouraged to learn more about this approach.

Transformative Classroom Management

Rather than assume that a problem, once identified, must be reacted to, and dealt with, transformative classroom management strives to determine the *source* of the problem and alter the source. Using this approach over time, managing the classroom changes things for the better for those who are within it—individuals and the collective all transform (i.e., change their nature). Classroom problems can be caused by teaching practices or by factors external to the classroom (Shindler, 2010). Examples include "the interaction between teacher or school and student, the systems in place, congruence between the expectations of the students and teachers, and the degree to which the class meets the students' basic needs" (Shindler, 2010, p. 6).

Transformative classroom management strategies include promoting (a) clear and shared classroom expectations; (b) a culture of listening, respect, and efficiency; (c) motivational strategies; (d) a success psychology in students; (e) a democratic classroom via a social contract and an ethos of student responsibility; (f) a cooperative and collaborative pedagogy; (g) a win-win approach to conflict and potential power struggles; and (h) a transformative mind set amongst students (Shindler, 2010). PSTs and novice teachers are encouraged to learn more about this approach, which is beyond the scope of this primer.

CHAPTER 5

AFTER CLASS

Assessing and Evaluating Student Learning

The ultimate goal of teaching is for students to learn. Thus, knowledge of both assessment and evaluation is necessary. *Assess* means to estimate (using incomplete information). *Evaluate* means to formally set a value for something using full(er) information (Harper, 2022). In educational settings, *assessment* is formative (as things are happening) and is focused on the learning *process* as it unfolds. *Evaluation* is summative (cumulatively adds things up) and happens afterwards. It involves making a *judgement* on learning success and progress by determining to what degree the learning goals, objectives, and outcomes were reached (Hitch & Youatt, 1995). A discussion of assessment versus evaluation (types and tools) is followed with an overview of marking versus grading. Assuming that teachers learn as they teach, the chapter ends with a comment about PSTs' self-reflection after preparing for and teaching each lesson.

TYPES OF ASSESSMENT

This primer focuses on three types of assessment: conventional, alternative, and performance. *Conventional* assessment is so named because it entails well-established approaches to gauging students' learning (i.e., the way things are usually done). *Alternative* assessment departs from the conventional, cognitive way of doing things with a stronger focus on affective learning. *Performance* assessment gives students a chance to apply what they have learned and tends to favour psychomotor learning (Cross, 1973; Florida State University [FSU], 2011; Janisch et al., 2007).

Learning to Teach: Primer on Teacher Education Methods, pp. 89–115
Copyright © 2024 by Information Age Publishing
www.infoagepub.com

Conventional Assessment

Conventional assessment comes in two forms: *objective* (not influenced by feelings or opinions) and *subjective* (influenced by feelings and opinions). *Objective* assessment requires learners to identify and select *the* correct response from several options or supply a word or short phrase to answer a question or complete a statement. There is a single, correct answer. Teachers often develop a master answer key to use when marking and grading. Examples of objective test instruments include multiple choice, true and false, fill in the blank, and matching (details to follow). *Subjective* tests permit learners to construct, organize, and present their *own* original answer. There is usually more than one answer and/or more than one way to express the right answer. Examples of subjective test instruments include short answer, essay, and extended response essay (details to follow) (Cross, 1973; Fleck, 1980; FSU, 2011).

Alternative Assessment

Alternative assessment strategies augment conventional assessment's concern for cognitive learning by focusing on students' affective learning informed by their worldviews, principles, values, attitudes, beliefs, and interests. How they learn and how that learning is progressing is deemed *just* as important as a one-time, objective snapshot for a specific assignment. Authentic (alternative) assessment thus concerns (a) students' strengths and weaknesses, (b) their individual growth over time, (c) their learning style(s), (d) their cultural and educational backgrounds and (e) how the learning experience helps them be self-reliant and self-reflective—traits that will serve them well into life (Janisch et al., 2007; Oxford Learning, 2017).

This assessment approach is called *authentic* (real, genuine) because learning is meaningful for students—what they learn will be useful in their real life. It *means* something to them (Janisch et al., 2007; Oxford Learning, 2017). Examples of authentic assessment strategies include service learning, project work, reflective journaling, and portfolios. These sorts of learning experiences can readily align with established learning outcomes and provide alternative but legitimate means of assessing students' proficiency in complex tasks. Such learning is realistic with assessment possible through rich avenues for judging the quality of learning (Bradley, 2021).

Performance Assessment

Sometimes teachers need to know if students can correctly perform certain tasks, actions, or functions (often the psychomotor domain), meaning they can carry them out successfully to certain standards: (a) safely function in a laboratory; (b) use a specific machine, tool, or piece of equipment; or (c) follow given steps, procedures, or other routines. Performance tests tend to measure skill, capability, accuracy, productivity, or application of principles in real-world settings or authentic simulations (Fleck, 1980; FSU, 2011).

When developing such assessment tools (e.g., demonstrations, events, student presentations), PSTs and novice teachers must (a) link the task to the learning outcomes and learning objectives; (b), clearly define the task that will be observed or rated; (c) specify the exact criteria constituting successful task completion; (d) set a specific time for the test or assessment (both when it will happen and time available for completion); and, to the best of their ability, (e) control and document the testing environment to ensure uniform testing for all students involved (Fleck, 1980; FSU, 2011).

Face and Content Validity of Assessment and Evaluation Tools

Assessment and evaluation tools (whether conventional, alternative, or performance) must meet at least two types of validity (i.e., be dependable on two fronts): face validity and content validity. First, the assessment tools must *appear* to others (on the face of things) as both (a) correlating with learning objectives and outcomes and (b) measuring course content (i.e., *face validity*). Second, the content of these tools must *actually be* related to learning objectives and outcomes and actually measure course content (i.e., *content validity*) (FSU, 2011).

Respectively, students should be able to see a connection between what they have studied and what they are being tested on, *and* the assessment tool must actually make that connection. Invalid assessment and evaluation tools compromise the evaluation process, wherein teachers determine if students have learned the intended course content (FSU, 2011).

Assessment and evaluation validity can be assured if PSTs and novice teachers respect some basic principles: (a) assessment is context dependent; (b) it means different things to different people; (c) students' attitudes toward assessment and evaluation can affect their motivation to learn; thus (d) evaluation depends on communicating to students the criteria and standards employed when assessing their learning progress (Walvoord & Anderson, 1998). The following text provides guidance on how to develop valid conventional (objective and subjective), alternative, and performance assessment tools. The roster is not inclusive, but it does reflect the most common and familiar tools that PSTs and novice teachers will encounter when delivering a top-down implemented curriculum, which remains the norm.

Conventional Objective Assessment Tools

Objective assessment (also called *limited-choice* assessment) serves the important role of assessing whether students have mastered the subject matter required to progress to the next level, or if they need to hone their knowledge base or competencies. These approaches are called *objective* because they are allegedly bias free (i.e., not influenced by the teacher's feelings, values, or personal opinions of the student). Thus, for each question, there is only *one* correct answer, and its rightness is not influenced by the teacher's bias. Granted, the particular questions asked on a test are not necessarily bias free, but the answers *are*. So is the grading process—there is only one right answer. The most popular objective tests are true/false, multiple choice, fill in the blank, and matching (Fleck, 1980; FSU, 2011).

True/False

This type of test item requires students to choose whether the statement is true or false. Students have a 50/50 chance of being right. Excessive guessing (i.e., making a choice with insufficient information) significantly lowers the validity of this type of test—did the test *really* measure what they know, or did it measure their ability to beat the probability odds—beat chance? Several strategies are useful for designing the best T/F test possible given its inherent weaknesses (Fleck, 1980; FSU, 2011; Hitch & Youatt, 1995):

- make items absolutely true or false.
- do not trick students. If not true, answers must be plausible (seeming reasonable), which in-the-know students will be able to spot.
- have at least 10 items in the test.
- either balance the number of true and false items or use 15% more false items because guessers tend to guess true more often than false.
- refer to only one idea in each item.
- use correct grammar.
- ask students to circle the letter T or F rather than write out the word in a blank.
- avoid negatives; if used, <u>underline</u> them.
- avoid sweeping terms (e.g., *all, may, always, never, often, usually, sometimes, none, few, less, more*); if used, include them in both false and true items.

- use the same number of words (or be the same length) for all items; it usually takes more words to prepare a false item—this can be a clue.
- avoid arranging items in a pattern (e.g., avoid TTT FFF TTT FFF).
- consider adding add a third choice *N* (not enough information) to determine whether students *know* there is not enough information to judge the statement as true or false.

In an interesting twist, Loveless and Betz (2021) provided tips for students to improve their true/false test scores. The test-development strategies listed above thus become test-taking strategies so students can *see* through them to better their performance in a game of chance.

Modified True/False. Appreciating that students have a 50/50 chance of guessing the correct answer in a conventional true/false test, the *modified* true/false test was developed. In addition to choosing true or false, students are further asked to justify or explain their choice in a written response. Some educators argue that asking students to explain their choice changes the test to a short answer type. Sometimes students can be asked to make a false statement true, if they chose false (Fleck, 1980; FSU, 2011).

Multiple Choice

As the name suggests, students have to *choose* the correct or most suitable answer from multiple (more than one) options. These tests are good for the cognitive domain of learning especially three levels: recall, understanding, and application. *If* they are well-prepared, multiple-choice tests can be very valid (i.e., measure what was intended), reliable (i.e., get same results if administered again) and able to discern who knows the intended content (Fleck, 1980; FSU, 2011; Hitch & Youatt, 1995).

Multiple choice questions comprise two parts: a *stem* (the main section that asks the question) and *items* (a list of possible responses or answers) (see Figure 5.1). Table 5.1 shares common tips for designing the best multiple-choice questions possible. PSTs must make sure they provide clear directions to students explaining how to answer the question (e.g., circle the correct letter) (Fleck, 1980; FSU, 2011; Hitch & Youatt, 1995).

Fill in the Blank

Also called a *completion* test, students are required to read a sentence and fill in any missing word(s), number(s), symbol(s), or formula(s). This test is

Figure 5.1

Example of a Multiple-Choice Question

Multiple Choice (circle the correct letter)

Which one of the following foods has the highest Vitamin C content?

A. Carrots

B. Milk

C. Oranges

D. Rice

E. Steak

Table 5.1

Guidelines for Designing Good Multiple-Choice Questions

Stem (contains the question)	**Items** (contains possible answers)
• pose a question rather than an incomplete. sentence. If a statement is used (no question mark), make it a complete sentence. • should be short and concise (one sentence, about 10–15 words). • stem is longer and more complex than items and requires precise wording. • include in the stem any words that might be repeated in the items (e.g., a, the, an, when). • be accurate in word choice because words have multiple meanings. • minimize use of negatively stated stems.	• have at least four items to choose from. • present items in a stacked list with each one identified with a letter or a number. • items must be grammatically correct and consistent (*ed, ing, ist, ion, s*) to minimize unintended clues. • make sure distractors (wrong answers) are plausible (reasonable). • keep all items close to the same length and the same level of difficulty. • mix up order of items from question to question (e.g., don't always make **"A"** the correct answer). • be wary of using "all of the above" or "none of the above" (encourages guessing). • avoid double negatives (i.e., "There isn't no other way"); instead, phrase positively (i.e., "There is no other way" or "There isn't another way").

especially good for measuring simple recall (i.e., remembering something that has been memorized). They work best for specific knowledge about major points of learning. When designing the test items, the first part of the sentence is the problem students will solve or answer. It can begin with one of several stems and related verbs: who (is/was), what (is/was), when (do/did/does), where (do/did/does), and why (do/did/does). Avoid sentence structure and grammar that give away the answer (e.g., *a, an, the*). Do not leave out so many words that the question is unanswerable or has too many feasible answers (i.e., it becomes ambiguous) (Cross, 1973; Fleck, 1980; Kelly, 2020).

The blank to be filled in should be at or near the end of the sentence. Blanks should be the same length in all questions and long enough for students to enter their handwritten or typed answer. The answer being sought should be limited to 1–3 words, but it can also be a symbol or a formula. A question can be posed with a blank that is placed after the question mark. Fill-in-the-blank tests can also be accompanied with a word list from which students choose their answers (Cross, 1973; Fleck, 1980; Kelly, 2020). Noteworthy is that a fill-in-the-blank (completion) test downplays guessing because it requires a definite response. Respecting this surety, questions should use familiar wording from the text or class materials (FSU, 2011) (see Figure 5.2 where the correct answer is in square brackets but would not be included in the actual test question).

Figure 5.2

Example of Fill-in-the-Blank Question

For the next four questions about playing baseball, fill in the blank with the word or number that best completes the sentence. Each answer is worth 1 point (5 points total).

1. Each baseball game normally has_____ innings. [9]
2. This many ball players from a team are fielded at one time. _____ [9]
3. The two people behind the home plate are called the _____ and the _____.
   [catcher and umpire]
4. A ball that goes out of bounds is called a _____ ball. [foul]

Matching

Matching questions are good for recall and for testing students' knowledge of relations between two ideas (e.g., Borscht is a dish made in Russia. Students would pair nation with food traditions and culture) (Fleck, 1980, FSU, 2011; Hitch & Youatt, 1995). In a testing environment, the word *matching* means a corresponding pair. Also called *recognition items*, these tests consist of a list of questions (premises) in the left column (prefaced with a number [1, 2, 3] and a blank line) and a list of answers (responses) in the right column (prefaced with a letter [A, B, C]). The two columns should be labelled as such (e.g., questions/premises, and responses/possible answers) (Fleck, 1980, FSU, 2011).

Students are asked to place the correct letter in the blank space beside the numbered question. They should be told if an answer (letter) can be used more than once. There should be at least 10 numbered questions (premises) in the left column. Because there should be more answers than premises (questions), the right column normally appears longer in length than the left. Having answers that are not used prevents an elimination process. Answers (right column) should be limited to 4–5 words. The entire question should be on one page (i.e., do not warp to next page). Avoid grammatical clues (Fleck, 1980, FSU, 2011) (see Figure 5.3 where the correct answer is in square brackets but would not be included in the actual test question).

Figure 5.3

Example of a Multiple-Choice Question

Directions: This question is about identifying fruits and vegetables. Write the correct or best answer (letter) from the right column in the blank space before a numbered statement on the left. There is one item (letter) left over. No item (letter) is used twice.

Premises (Questions)	Responses (Possible Answers)
____ 1. This fruit is round and orange. [C]	A. Carrot
____ 2. This vegetable is long and orange. [A]	B. Banana
____ 3. This vegetable is oblong and white. [E]	C. Orange
____ 4. This fruit is long and yellow. [B]	D. Turnip
	E. Potato

Per Figure 5.3, this was purposively not the best example. It helps illustrate how the directions do not clarify that the color refers to the outside of the food and not the inside. **E** is the intended answer for **3**, *but* potatoes can also be round, oddly shaped, and colors other than white on the outside (brown, yellow, red, blue, and green if sunburned). Also, some turnips are oblong (tubular) and white (meaning **D** could be used for question **3**), but they always have a second band of color (normally purple). They are an off-white, beige color inside. These ambiguities create confusion and illustrate how the validity of the test question can easily be compromised.

Conventional Subjective Assessment Tools

Subjective assessment tools (also called *open-ended testing*) give students a chance to express their learning in their *own* words. Students use the opportunity to organize and present an original answer. It is called *subjective* because answers are based on students' personal interpretations, feelings, tastes, and opinions combined with cognition (what they know and their thinking abilities). Subjective answers are dependent on the student's mind for existence while objective answers are dependent on the facts. Scoring and grading are also subjective in that they can be influenced by both the teachers' emotions and mood (e.g., bored, tired, frustrated, or hungry) and their feelings or opinions about the student (Fleck, 1980; FSU, 2011). Subjective tests include short answer, essay, and restricted and extended response essays.

Short Answer

Compared to a lengthy essay, answers to short-answer questions are about 2–3 full sentences in length, a short paragraph (3–5 full sentences or 150 words), or even just a phrase. The question itself is one complete sentence. The answer is short because the usual intent is to recall information (cognitive domain of learning). The question should not be ambiguous or open to multiple interpretations. When posing it, PSTs should provide guidelines on what they want students to write about. In other words, specify the conditions (e.g., provide three reasons for something, restrict your answer to three sentences, outline your answers in point form). Pragmatically, if appropriate, leave enough space for students to handwrite or type their answers (Fleck, 1980; FSU, 2011; Hitch & Youatt, 1995) (see Figure 5.4).

Figure 5.4

Examples of Short Answer Questions

---

1. By providing at least four facts, *describe* the difference between a river-front cottage and a beach front cottage. Restrict your answer to two paragraphs.
2. *Compare* and *contrast* a flower and a maple leaf in terms of both structure and function. Answer should be about 150 words.
3. *Identify* and *explain* three key elements of informed consent when taking part in a research study. Keep answer to five sentences.

Essay

Despite their disadvantages (e.g., hard to mark, long to mark, and very subjective grading), essays are a powerful way to "allow expression of both breadth and depth of learning, and encourage originality, creativity, and divergent thinking" (FSU, 2011, p. 159). They are an excellent way to test higher order thinking and levels of reasoning because they often require students to (a) muster then logically and clearly organize their ideas and (b) make inferences, comparisons, and contrasts (Fleck, 1980). Students get a chance to express what they know along with their beliefs, values, and powers of argument. Essays are also useful for synthesizing a broad (comprehensive) base of information at the end of a module or the course itself (FSU, 2011; Hitch & Youatt, 1995; Kelly, 2019a).

The essay question should clearly identify exactly what students are supposed to do, what topic to address, and within what parameters (i.e., measurable characteristics). Tell them how long it should be (normally 2–3 hand-written pages if an in-class exam) and specify grading criteria: (a) accuracy of facts (course content); (b) clarity of writing (choice, organization, and sequencing of ideas; choice and use of vocabulary; progression of thinking; technical aspects of writing); and (c) persuasiveness of argument. If the essay question has multiple parts, advise students of each part's value (20%, 30%, 50%). The first word of the question is often a verb from Bloom's taxonomy of learning for the cognitive domain (see Table 3.4) (Fleck, 1980; FSU, 2011) and should be aligned with one or more previously specified learning outcomes or objectives. Sometimes it is useful to define the verb associated with the learning outcome (Hitch & Youatt, 1995) (see Figure 5.5).

Figure 5.5

Example of an Essay Question

"In 2–3 pages, elaborate on how historians Mary Jones and Adam White differed on their opinions on mandatory school lunches in local school boards." Elaborate means to carefully write something up by providing, and fully developing, several details. You will be marked on your recall of course information (50%) and the strength of your elaboration (50%).

Regarding the students' answer, because of the subjective nature of this assessment tool, there is no real *right* answer to an essay question. But to better ensure that the test is valid (i.e., measures both subject-matter content and students' thinking and argumentation prowess), PSTs and novice teachers are encouraged to write a model answer themselves and use that as a key when marking and grading students' essays. This key provides parameters for what the PST thinks the students *should* know, content wise at least. If the essay is an exam question during a class (rather than a take-home or end-of-term assignment), teachers must remain very aware of time constraints – both students' time for completion and teacher's marking time to promptly return feedback (Fleck, 1980; Kelly, 2019a).

Restricted and Extended Response Essays

Some educators distinguish between restricted and extended response essay questions. Restrict means to hold back. Extend means to stretch out (Anderson, 2014). Restricted response essays literally limit students' answers to very clear parameters. Kelly (2019a, para. 2) provided the following example: "*State the main differences between John Adams' and Thomas Jefferson's beliefs about federalism.*" Students know they cannot expand or extend their answer beyond how these two particular people's views differed on one particular topic. Restricted response essay questions are good for discerning students' abilities to synthesize and organize course material (Kelly, 2019a).

Extended response essay questions give students the chance to step back and choose what they think is necessary and useful to answer the question. They are given an overall topic and are free to use their own judgement about what course content and what from of argumentation best helps form their opinion expressed in their response (Kelly, 2019a). She offered this example. "*In John Steinbeck's book* Of Mice and Men, *do you think George's killing of Lennie was justified? Explain your answer*" (Kelly, 2019a, para. 3). These types of questions are good for discerning students' abilities to judge and evaluate something using information they were supposed to learn during the course (Kelly, 2019a).

Alternative, Authentic Assessment Tools

A learning task is authentic when (a) students construct their own responses instead of selecting from teacher-provided ones and (b) the task replicates challenges in their real world (Mueller, 2023). Those fortunate enough to experience a bottom-up enactment curriculum (or a progressive, top-down implementation curriculum) may have the opportunity to employ various authentic assessment tools that place learning in the students' hands with the teacher acting as a facilitator, coach, and guide or some combination (Collins & O'Brien, 2003). Students gain opportunities to problem solve, experiment, investigate, critique, explore, inquire, reflect, and even serve their community. This approach is miles beyond rote memorization and mastery of subject matter content, which is perpetu-ated using the conventional, objective testing protocol.

Three common authentic tools are profiled herein: portfolios, projects, and project-based learning (PBL), and service learning. Other examples beyond the scope of this primer include simulations, students' perfor-mances (e.g., music or dance), debates, dialogue circles, role playing, mock conferences, mock parliaments, laboratory experiments (see Chapter 4), young writer's programs, exhibitions and demonstrations, fashion shows, and case study analyses (Mueller, 2023).

Portfolios

Portfolio is Latin *portafoglio*, "movable case for carrying detached papers" (Harper, 2022). In educational practice, a portfolio is set of pieces of cre-ative work intended to demonstrate the student's abilities or achievements or to convince others something was learned (Anderson, 2014; Birgin & Baki, 2007). Brown (1995) best described a portfolio as "a private collection of evidence, which demonstrates the continuing acquisition of skills, knowl-edge, attitudes, understanding and achievements. It is both retrospective and prospective, as well as reflecting the current stage of development and activity of the individual" (p. 3). Retrospective means looking back on past events or situations (e.g., self-evaluation as well as critical reflection of what is in the portfolio and what it means). Prospective means looking forward by adjusting existing or framing new intended learning goals or expressing what is envisioned for one's future learning (Janisch et al., 2007).

At the beginning of the course, the PST or novice teacher should explain the concept of a portfolio to students (perhaps show an example) and instruct them to prepare a collection of learning artifacts to convince the teacher of their learning. Portfolios are intended to demonstrate current knowledge and skills that emerge as students' learning progresses over the course (Birgin & Baki, 2007). They can contain in-class work, artwork, textiles or other constructions, written essays, videos, films, podcasts, pho-tographs, tangible items, PowerPoints, and other media. Teachers should also advise students that they will be expected to select the *best* evidence of their learning from this collection and prepare a reflection on why they think each piece is *the* best evidence that they have learned something (Brown, 1995; Meador, 2019).

Student-centered learning experiences like portfolios help learners both develop more positive attitudes about learning in general and take control of their learning. But it is equally acceptable for the student and teacher to collaboratively decide what pieces should be included with the student making the final decision (with justification) and the teacher acting as guide and facilitator. Because portfolios inadvertently enable students to mask weaknesses in certain learning areas (e.g., they can choose to leave out poorly done artifacts), teachers do need to remain somewhat involved in decisions about what is included for evaluation (Birgin & Baki, 2007; FSU, 2011; Janisch et al., 2007; Meador, 2019).

Portfolios are especially good for helping students "formulate deeper understandings of the concepts they are learning beyond a simple [one-test] surface explanation" (Meador, 2019, para. 11). Portfolios encourage extended thinking and reasoning and provide opportunities to express many ways of knowing (FSU, 2011). Not surprisingly, teachers soon discover that marking portfolios is time consuming, and grading is challenging because portfolios are *so* subjective. What the student perceives as authentic for him or her (*real* learning) may not convince the teacher that the student has learned or mastered course content. Thus, teachers must decide what the portfolio must contain to be considered a learning success and deserving of a passing grade and share this information with students beforehand (Meador, 2019).

This advice to students should be further augmented with directions about (a) the expected number of artifacts, (b) their nature, (c) their quality (likely explained using a rubric) and (d) the physical size of the actual portfolio (FSU, 2011). In short, a "portfolio is a fusion of process and product. It is the process of reflection, selection, rationalization, and evaluation, together with the product of those processes" (Winsor & Ellefson, 1995, p. 68).

Project-Based Learning

"Authentic assessment is a form of assessment in which students are asked to perform real-world tasks that demonstrate meaningful application of essential knowledge and skills" (Sambeka et al., 2017, p. 2). A prime example of this is project-based learning (PBL). Project is Late Latin *projectare*, "to thrust forward; to plan, to scheme" (Harper, 2022). A project is a carefully planned undertaking (individual or collaborative) to achieve a particular goal (Anderson, 2014) (e.g., a learning goal). PBL is also the acronym for problem-based learning. Some educators understand project-based as students completing an artifact to demonstrate content mastery and problem-based as presenting a solution to an authentic problem. Herein PBL refers to both approaches because students must use course content to solve the problem.

To complete the project, students work over an extended period of time (often the entire course) to learn about a complex question, challenge, or problem by using inquiry, investigation, experimentation, research, and reflection. As fully explained by Solomon (2003, p. 1),

> in project-based learning, students work [alone or] in groups to solve challenging problems that are authentic, curriculum-based, and often interdisciplinary. Learners decide how to approach a problem and what activities to pursue. They gather information from a variety of sources and synthesize, analyze, and derive knowledge from it. Their learning is inherently valuable because it's connected to something real and involves adult skills such as collaboration and reflection. At the end, students demonstrate their newly acquired knowledge and are judged by how much they've learned and how well they communicate it. Throughout this process, the teacher's role is to guide and advise, rather than to direct and manage, student work.

Projects "engage students through hands-on, serious, authentic experiences. They also allow for alternative approaches that address students' individual differences, variations in learning styles, intelligences, abilities, and disabilities" (Solomon, 2003, p. 1). Students demonstrate their learning by presenting (i.e., thrusting forward) their results to the public—their classroom, maybe their school (e.g., science fairs) or to a real audience (e.g., fashion shows or industry fairs and exhibits). Examples of PBL include (a) testing water samples and sharing information with an environmental agency or (b) redesigning a community center in consultation with city administrators.

When students realize that their academic work is valuable for addressing real-world issues (i.e., authentic), and that their work can impact real lives (i.e., meaningful), they become more motivated and empowered to learn (Solomon, 2003). As with portfolios, projects tend to be graded using teacher and student cocreated rubrics (to be discussed) as well as student self-assessment and sometimes peer assessment (peer review), which is a structured learning process wherein students critique and provide feedback on each others' work (Sambeka et al., 2017).

Service Learning

As the name implies, students *learn* outside the classroom by providing a *service* to their community via acts of assistance. They *learn in service* to others. Service learning integrates course-based learning with both community service and student self-reflections (McGregor, 2002). In short, "students conduct research on [or with] their community to identify needs, prioritize areas of greatest needs, select needs they can help meet, design a project, provide the service, and reflect before, throughout and after the project" (McGregor, 2002, p. 43). Service-learning examples include designing and building urban community gardens; creating recycling programs; providing food, clothing, and shelter for people without a home (e.g., the homeless); designing neighborhood playgrounds; teaching or tutoring underprivileged children; creating wheelchair ramps; or completing a community history project (McGregor, 2002).

While learning in service, students will encounter events that (a) confirm or conflict with their assumptions of the world and their place within it and (b) challenge their current understandings of life leading perhaps to perplexity and dissonance (doubt, conflicting beliefs) (McGregor, 2002). Because students' community embeddedness while learning might expose them to societal inadequacies and injustices, teachers must create a quiet space within the course for students to decompress, reflect on their actions, delve into self-awareness, and wrestle with speculation and questions (de Acosta, 1995).

PSTs and novice teachers can use an array of assessment tools to formally evaluate student success with service learning, so they can mark and assign a grade: preservice activity plans; observation checklists; rating scales (self, teacher, peers, and onsite supervisors); rubrics; portfolios; and student journaling and self-reflections (Davis et al., 1998). Aside from the strategies already described in this chapter, examples are available at Davis et al. (1998) and elsewhere. The intent is for PSTs and novice teachers to collect enough data to judge the quality of the service-learning experience as it pertains to students' academic achievement per course learning goals and learning objectives.

Performance Assessment Tools

Tools designed to *assess performance* involve students actually demonstrating the skills (doing real-world tasks) that the test is designed to measure instead of answering questions about how to do it. Performance tests require students to (a) apply a particular skill set and use specific knowledge for which they have received instruction in class in conjunction with (b) critical thinking and creative, strategic problem solving. Beyond rote memorization, students have to work independently and must pay attention to that work and its quality to satisfy their teacher that the learning objective(s) were achieved (Hibbard et al.,1996; Vander Ark, 2013).

Examples of performance assessment tools include dramatic performances, dance or music recitals, sports performances, projects and project-based learning, video-game simulations (e.g., flight simulators), laboratories, and portfolios. Indeed, performance assessment tools often veer into the realm of alternative assessment because they involve displays of learning in authentic, real-world settings or close simulations (Hibbard et al., 1996; Vander Ark, 2013) (see previous section for details about port-folios, projects, and PBL).

TYPES OF EVALUATION

As noted, assessment and evaluation are related but different. Students complete and pass in assignments and tests designed by the teacher (see previous section on assessment), who then judges (evaluates) them for their quality. This *evaluation* (i.e., judging the quality of students' assessments) can occur along three trajectories: (a) norm-referenced standards (compare a student to other students); (b) criterion-referenced standards (compare a student to an independent, preset standard); and (c) self-referenced standards (compare a student against their own past achievements) (FSU, 2011). To illustrate,

> for the student who scores 90 marks, for example, norm-referenced feed-back could be: 'Very good, you are the top student in the class.' When giving criterion-referenced feedback, you might say, 'Very good, you have mas-tered nearly all that I have taught.' Or it could be self-referenced feedback: 'Very good, you have achieved better results as compared to your last test.' (Youyan et al., 2013, paras. 10, 11)

Norm-Referenced Standard

With the norm-referenced standard, a student is compared against other students' knowledge of course content. The *norm* is the performance typical of their peer group. This approach (for good or bad) encourages competition and perpetuates a win-lose attitude, which, if not balanced with cooperative and collaborative learning, can have its downsides. Dis-appointed and anxious students feeling competitive pressure can lose motivation to learn, negative relationships can emerge between or among fellow students, and students may lack information and feedback about how they can personally improve their own learning. All they know is how they did compared to others (Gross Davis, 1999).

Hand in hand with the norm-referenced standard is *grading on the curve*—a statistical approximation of the *norm* (expected average) for an entire class. Individual student's legitimate grades can be affected by outli-ers (see Figure 5.6). For example, if too many people scored more than 75, when the expected average test score was 50, students who actually earned 75 may see their score lowered significantly when grades are reported. It could be that the test was too easy, or maybe the teacher was so good that all students earned >75 (FSU, 2011). Regardless, some students are dis-advantaged when graded on the curve.

Figure 5.6

Grading on the Curve

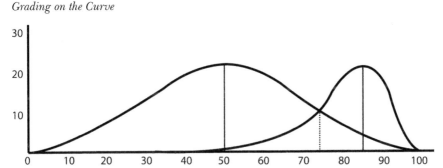

Criterion-Referenced Standard

Criterion-referenced standards are associated with students being compared to preset *criteria* for being able to think, do, or feel in a certain, predetermined way. One student's grade is not affected by other students' performance nor the calibre of the class—the norm (FSU, 2011).

Alpha, Numeric, and Grade Point Average (GPA)

A common example of a preset criterion grading and marking experience would be the use of an alpha grade strategy wherein any numeric score between 90 and 100 equates to **A+** (for example). A final grade of 89 (off by one digit) would be scored lower at **A** because someone has arbitrarily decided beforehand what constitutes an A versus an A+ (FSU, 2011). Fortunately, if students are informed ahead of time about the differences, they can gain insights into how to improve their learning. The predetermined standards (criterion-referenced) distinguish among *letter grades* (A [alpha], B [beta], C [gamma], D [delta], and F [fail]) or *Grade Point Average* (GPA) scores with established adjectives and narratives. Depending on the educational institution, GPAs range from 0–4 or from 0–4.3 with 3.0 or 3.3 respectively considered an average score.

Table 5.2 explains the alpha grade and GPA approaches with information culled from many higher education institutions' registrars' offices. Table 5.2 must be read in its entirety. In my own teaching practice, I distributed this document to PSTs at the very beginning of a course and then used it to mark and grade their academic work. This way there were no surprises when grades were assigned at the end of the course. Students knew ahead of time the criteria (standards) against which they their work would be referenced (criterion-referenced). They could strive to work to that standard if they chose to do so.

Table 5.2

Alpha, Grade Point Average (GPA), and Numeric Grades With Attendant Narratives

"A" Range (A+ A A-) Outstanding - Exceptional - Excellent Performance
A+ Outstanding GPA 4.3 (90–100) You have a rare talent for the subject. Your work demonstrated a very rich, exciting, comprehensive, and full understanding of the course concepts even the subject area. You illustrated outstanding interpretive and analytical ability and originality. Your work reflected unforgettable intellectual engagement and initiative—an incisive mind. There was considerable evidence of original, reflective thinking, and an ability to synthesize ideas. There was no question of the depth of your knowledge base as it relates to the course material and how it relates to other disciplines. Your use of theory and ideologies to express your ideas was insightful and inspiring. Your work was superior to others—even *distinguished* in its caliber. Your ideas even went so far as to contribute to theoretical and philosophical arguments thanks to your original interpretations. Your work more than surpassed the expectations for the course—you *stand out* from all others.
A Exceptional GPA 4.0 (85–89) Your work demonstrated a superior grasp of the subject matter and content with development of relevant concepts and skills at a high level. Your work was far above others in quality and excellence and far above what is usual or normal for this grade level. Your work was indicative of a high level of interpretive and analytical ability reflecting intellectual initiative that is the exception not the rule. Your work will attract the notice of others because it reflected a growing degree of ingenuity and interpretation of research and readings. Indeed, your work came close to surpassing the expectations for the course. It was *the exception* (unusually good) not the rule.
A- Excellent GPA 3.7 (80–84) *A-* means excellent work (excelled, well above average) that is comprehensive and accurate. Evidence of a certain flair for, and comprehension of, the entire subject was clearly perceptible. Your work reflected a thorough knowledge of the course materials with some exceptions. It indicated that you have taken advantage of the opportunities in class and found ways to use some of the course material in new and creative ways in and perhaps outside of class. You have shown that you understand some facets of the course material in your life and school context and the significance of the learnings. As well, you have shown that you have a good appreciation for how the material relates to other areas of knowledge by making interdisciplinary connections. Your grasp of the content and concepts was deeply thorough at this point in time, and you were striving for creative ways to illustrate this. There were instances where your thinking could have been stretched further, but your work showed that you were taking critical stances in relation to the underlying assumptions of the field of study. Your work surpassed and *excelled* that of others in the class.

(Table continued on next page)

Table 5.2 (Continued)

Alpha, Grade Point Average (GPA), and Numeric Grades With Attendant Narratives

"B" Range (B+ B B-) Very Good - Good - Acceptable Performance (Continued)
B+ Very Good GPA 3.3 (77–79) You thoroughly met the course expectations, demonstrated a thorough understanding of the course material (at least the content that you used or applied), and you performed above the expected standard. There was some evidence of critical thinking and a developing understanding of some relevant issues from the course, even theoretical and ideological assumptions, but not to the higher degree evident in A level work. Some of the work was quite carefully done while other parts were less critical. Some parts of the work reflected a certain flair for the content of the course while others did not. You're thinking about the content of the course was becoming more organized, and you were making progress toward comprehending its essential core. You are *beginning* to appreciate how the material relates to other areas of knowledge and practice. The work was tantalizing and proof that you are capable of deeper intellectual engagement with the ideas.
B Good GPA 3.0 (73–76) You have a moderate grasp of the overarching goals of the course. You met the expected standard, the learning intended for the course. Overall, you performed at a level that illustrates careful, craftsman-like competency; but too many valuable insights were missing because your analysis was not yet rigorous enough. There was evidence in your work that you had grasped some areas of the course in more detail than others. I am left with a sense of uncertainty of your *complete* understanding of the course, which demanded more rigorous, deeper, and synergistic thinking than is usually evident in B+ quality work. There were bursts of intellectual insights, but a consistent, deeper grasp of the course content was not yet evident. That is, you showed evidence of some intellectual initiative and some originality but not consistently. You have clear potential to pursue higher levels of thinking and intellectual integration, but you are not there just yet.
B- Acceptable GPA 2.7 (70–72) The work you put forth is intellectually *adequate* for this course. Your use of the key or essential concepts of the course was competent but usually underdeveloped. I am not yet convinced that you have developed a solid, conceptual framework reflective of the content that shaped the course. Your course work reflected a moderate quality contribution that is sufficient, but not more so. The B- grade indicates respectable development of relevant skills and modes of thinking to a passable level, but more intellectual engagement and reflection is absent and required. The academic work was acceptable, meaning it was stronger than the minimum level required, but it still needs improvement.

(Table continued on next page)

Table 5.2 (Continued)

Alpha, Grade Point Average (GPA), and Numeric Grades With Attendant Narratives

"C" Range (C+ C C-) GPA 1.7–2.3 (60–69) Competent Performance, Satisfactory Without Excess
C range work indicates fulfilment of the *minimum* course requirements (least amount of work possible or attainable) with a fair demonstration of the material. It reflected just a competent standard (satisfactory without excess) with a particular part of the course but not with all parts. Especially, a C range grade indicates incompleteness and usually inaccuracies (errors and omissions). Furthermore, your work may have demonstrated an incomplete understanding of the course content, nature of the assignment, level of analysis required for the assignment or course, or some combination. This could have happened because you were only *familiar* with the literature, set readings and course content and had not yet engaged with them on a sufficient intellectual level. Your work reflected an ability to develop less-complex lines of thinking and suggested that you were not challenging yourself enough. There was little evidence of independent thought and initiative.

"D" GPA 1 (50–59) Poor Performance (Underperformance)
Your work reflected an underperformance overall (worse than expected) with the weaknesses outweighing any strengths evident in the scholarship. You barely fulfilled the requirements of the course (the essential learnings). Your academic work was of low, inferior quality and standard, and it lacked intellectual rigour or sophistication. Although D is a passing grade (the lowest passing grade), it is given for work that is only marginally acceptable (almost insufficient—on the brink of not passing) for one or more reasons: consistent poor performance on tests or assignments (intimating you had not learned the content); late, missed, or poorly executed assignments; less-than-required class participation and contributions; or excessive absences or tardiness (meaning lost opportunities to be exposed to and engage with course content and learnings). A *poor* grade means you barely managed to grasp even the basics of the course material because you were underperforming.

"F" GPA 0 (0–49) Failure, Insufficient, Inadequate (Nonperformance)
An F grade indicates failure. It reflects an unsatisfactory (unacceptable) performance because of some combination of an (a) inadequate understanding of the basic subject matter (scant, very limited accumulation of subject-related knowledge); (b) inability to demonstrate an adequate grasp of the material (inadequate discipline-related information base), *especially* the main theories, constructs, concepts and/or principles; (c) inability to develop or demonstrate relevant skills or competencies; (d) insufficient evidence of interpretive abilities (unable to provide various explanations) and analytical abilities (no originality in conjunction with confused, uncritical thinking); (e) little or no evidence of reference to important concepts or issues pertinent to the subject matter; and/or (f) inability to achieve even minor course learning goals or learning objectives set out in the course outline.

(Table continued on next page)

Table 5.2 (Continued)

Alpha, Grade Point Average (GPA), and Numeric Grades With Attendant Narratives

"F" GPA 0 (0–49) Failure, Insufficient, Inadequate (Nonperformance)
In writing assignments, there were considerable faults in style, grammar, syntax, punctuation, and the like. There might be weak signs of an argument (your position on a topic or issue), but these signs were obscured by faulty logic, incoherent presentation and organization, and syntax errors (mistakes in the arrangement of words in sentences, the order used to present ideas). Because you're writing and presentation of ideas were barely comprehensible, it was difficult to assess what you intended as the main message of the assignment, and thus difficult to discern if you had learned the course content. If the course involved a practicum or internship, your behavior and performance were incompatible with accepted practice or with de rigueur problem-solving approaches (did not conform to accepted [and expected] standards of practice, possibly resulting in unsafe or irresponsible behavior). You may have exhibited a limited understanding of major and ethical issues of the discipline's approach to practice.

Rubrics

Rubrics are another example of criterion-referenced assessment. Rubric is Latin *rubrica terra*, "red earth or ochre writing material." It is also Old French *rubrique*, "directions in religious services, often written in red ink" (Anderson, 2014; Harper, 2022). In the education arena, rubrics provide *directions* for students relative to different degrees of completing an assignment. Teachers traditionally mark assignments using *red* ink. To wit, rubrics are a set of instructions or rules (directions) for how to achieve something, in this case a particular grade on a specific assignment. Teachers prepare rubrics ahead of time (ideally with students), so students know to what standard they have to work to get a particular mark (FSU, 2011). Astute students will use the rubric to improve their learning by striving to achieve the highest number of points.

Presented in matrix form, the left column of a rubric usually contains the criteria, and the other columns contain degrees of performance. Each criterion row has narrative in each cell for specific levels of performance with designated points earned (FSU, 2011). In Figure 5.7, there are four criteria and four levels of performance for each criterion. Using this rubric, scores on a writing assignment can range from 16 points (highest score) to 4 points (lowest score).

Figure 5.7

Example of a Rubric to Grade a Writing Assignment

Criteria	A *Outstanding* (far exceeds standard) 4	B *Above Average* (exceeds standard) 3	C *Satisfactory* (meets standard) 2	D *Inadequate* (below standard) 1
Organization, Reasoning, and Logic	*Writing draws in and intrigues the reader; very high degree of reasoning, logic, and argumentation; smooth transition among ideas; everything convincingly holds together*	*Writing is coherent and logically organized; acceptable reasoning and effective transitioning between and unity among ideas*	*While writing is coherent and logically organized, some ideas are misplaced; reasoning is weak but sufficient; transitions, although evident, are not effectively used throughout*	*Writing lacks organization and coherence; lack of transition statements and flaws in logic make it difficult for reader to follow the argument*
Quality of Writing Assignment's Content	*Content shows original thought, in depth analysis, and synthesis of ideas with irrefutable support and evidence for the topic*	*Content usually shows original thinking, some degree of analysis and synthesis with sufficient and firm evidence*	*Some ideas reflect original thinking and deep analysis, but there is little synthesis and often insufficient evidence*	*Many ideas are underdeveloped, not original and do not reflect solid analysis nor is there support for ideas being developed*
Critical Thinking and Development of Ideas	*Very high degree of thinking critically; main points are very well developed—both their quantity and quality*	*Main points are present with better-than-expected level of critical thinking; evidence of high degree of quantity and quality of idea development*	*Main points are present with some evidence of critical thinking; limited development of several points—both quantity and details*	*Several main points are missing; what is there lacks detail with nominal evidence of critical thinking*
Grammar and Mechanics	*Correct use of spelling, punctuation, and syntax; very smooth and enjoyable read*	*A few spelling, punctuation, and syntax errors; still easy to follow ideas*	*Some mistakes in spelling, syntax, and punctuation; moderately distracting but can usually follow ideas*	*Many spelling, punctuation, and syntax mistakes; distracting and very difficult to read; very challenging to follow ideas*

Self-Referenced Standard

Finally, the self-referenced standard entails comparing a student's academic performance improvement against their own past progress and academic achievements or expectations of same. Instead of the rest of the class or some predetermined external standard, students are compared to themselves so teachers and students can monitor the latter's progress over time. Students look back on their own performance using internal *norms* (i.e., their own standards or known/perceived abilities) and ponder "*Have I improved, how, and how much*?" Also, teachers may track an individual student's progress and compare current performance with their past relative to what the teacher thinks the student is capable of achieving (McColskey & Leary, 1985; Youyan et al., 2013).

Rubrics are often used for self-referenced standard assessment (Bradley, 2021). They can be both informative and evaluative. Regarding the former, rubrics are especially powerful if the PST or novice teacher can temporarily "disconnect them from grades and give students time and support to revise their work" (Bradley, 2021, para. 1) as they learn and move forward. When this pressure is removed, students can better appreciate the varying levels of quality set out in the rubric and position themselves to gauge how they have improved or can self-improve (Andrade, 2008).

MARKING AND GRADING

PSTs and novice teachers must learn how to mark and grade students' academic work. Although often used interchangeably, these two terms are different. Some educators assume that students earn *marks* (scores) on each element of a course's evaluation scheme. To illustrate, there might be three elements: two midterms (35%), a term paper (25%) and a final exam (40%). The final *grade* for the course would be the total of all the individual *marks* (e.g., 75% or B) (FSU, 2011; Seth, 2003).

This primer augments this perspective by assuming that marking and grading refer to different *mental activities* on behalf of the teacher. Marking equates to PSTs *reading* students' output, while grading equates to *judging* it. Marking is objective, and grading is subjective. Marking pertains to *measuring* learning progress by collecting different types of data from different sources that reflect students' learning comprehension and academic progress. Grading entails *judging* the quality of these data against criteria and standards and then assigning or awarding a grade (e.g., number, letter, pass/fail) for both the individual assignment and the entire course (Blakenship & Moerchen, 1979; Gross Davis, 1999; Hitch & Youatt, 1995). Table

5.2 (alpha, numeric, and GPAs) will help with these subjective judgements. Although best suited to the junior high/middle school, and secondary level, primary grade PSTs and novice teachers can gain insights from Table 5.2 as well.

Answer Keys for Objective Tests

PSTs and novice teachers should prepare an answer key beforehand to use when grading objective tests (e.g., matching, fill in the blanks). This key usually involves writing the answers on a paper copy of the test. Key answers can be (a) the only correct answer or (b) the teacher's idea of the best answer of several possible ones. The answer key should be piloted (dry run) before giving the test to students and edited or corrected accordingly to better ensure validity and reliability. Once prepared, the answer key should be kept current and reflect changes to any reused tests (Cross, 1973; Ernst, 2020; FSU, 2011).

Analytical Scoring

Someone once jokingly told me to throw all the essays down a flight of stairs. The ones at the bottom would get the highest scores because they were the heaviest (i.e., contained the most knowledge). Thankfully, a range of credible strategies has been developed for subjective assessments with special attention to analytic scoring and holistic scoring (especially for essays and extended response essays). When opting for analytic scoring, the PST or novice teacher should (a) identify the grading criteria, (b) specify polar opposites for each criterion on a continuum (e.g., accurate to inaccurate) with a numeric score range (e.g., 4–0), (c) prioritize the criteria and, finally, (d) assign relative weights out of 100% (see Figure 5.8).

This approach is called analytical because it involves an *analysis* of both the elements of and overall structure of the essay. In Figure 5.8, the total 100 is achieved by converting each criterion's score on a **5**-point scale (4, 3, 2, 1, 0 means five possible scores) to a percentage mark. To illustrate, for criterion 1, a student's score of 4 on a **5**-point scale equates to 5/5x30=30%. For criterion 2 (20%), a student's score of 0 equates to 0/5x20=0% and so on (FSU, 2011). If someone scored 100% on the essay assignment, the teacher judged the quality of their work to be accurate, insightful, and succinct with their arguments clearly articulated, well-supported, organized, and readable.

Figure 5.8

Analytical Scoring Scale (adapted from FSU, 2011)

Criteria:		Scale (five possible points):				
Respective Weights:		4	3	2	1	0
1. Ability to correctly recognize main points	30%	Accurate--------------------------Inaccurate				
2. Ability to distinguish between two positions	20%	Insightful ----------------------------Vague				
3. Ability to summarize	10%	Succinct --------------Too much/too little				
4. Ability to clearly articulate one's own position	5%	Clear-------------------------------Confusing				
5. Ability to support position taken using information from assigned readings	15%	Adequate, logical,------------Inadequate, refers to articles illogical, ignores articles				
6. Organization and readability	20%	Organized,--------------------Unorganized, well-communicated confusing to read				
Total Weight	**100%**					

Source: FSU (2011).

Holistic Scoring

Holistic scoring involves a different strategy. It is so named because each essay is judged in its entirety (the *whole* thing) after comparing it to an anchor paper (key) written by the teacher rather than each essay being analyzed for a collection of criteria specified by the teacher (analytical, see left side of Figure 5.8). In the holistic approach, instructors are encouraged to prepare three model essays (i.e., answer keys) representing good, fair, and poor responses to the assignment (with attendant score ranges) and then read and compare each student's essay to these models (anchors) (FSU, 2011; Nordquist, 2019).

A second holistic approach is to first read each student's essay to get an overall impression (i.e., holistic overview). When done reading, place it in a stack reflecting good, fair, or poor responses (or perhaps outstanding, above average, satisfactory, and inadequate—see Figure 5.7). Then, read each stack in its entirety (e.g., the poor response stack) so that likeminded levels of performance are read together. Assign grades for each stack or assign a grade for each essay in that stack within a range (perhaps using Table 5.2) (FSU, 2011; Nordquist, 2019).

A third strategy is to first read all essays to discern if students perform low on any *particular* course *material* and then grade individual essays accordingly appreciating that the teaching was likely at fault for that particular content (Fleck, 1980). In a fourth approach for multisection essays, teachers are encouraged to read all responses to each section (for all the essays) and assign a section grade for each student before moving onto the next section. Repeat this until done reading and grading all sections of the essay for everyone. Then tally the section marks for, and award a grade to, *each* student's essay (FSU, 2011).

Regardless of the approach being used (analytic or holistic), PSTs and novice teachers should stop marking (reading) when they are tired, hungry, irritable, or bored. When they resume marking, they should reread the last few papers to ensure fairness and adjust marks accordingly. They are also encouraged to conceal students' identity before reading to better ensure some degree of objectivity in a very subjective mode of assessment (FSU, 2011). This rule stands unless the self-reference standard is being applied, and the student's identity is necessary to gauge their progress.

Rubrics for Marking and Grading Essays

Rubrics (previously discussed) are very helpful for grading subjective assessments like essays. The criteria in the rubric should allow PSTs to discern students' degree of engagement with course material wherein they express their knowing in writing (Bradley, 2021; FSU, 2011). Used this way, rubrics would be designed so teachers can check that the essay contains sufficient course content to show that students have met the learning outcomes. In the essay, students will establish a clear controlling idea (i.e., their opinion) that they intend to develop about the essay topic. Students will exhibit logical progression from one thought to another so teachers can sense their ability to both (a) develop their opinion and (b) prove they have a thorough understanding of the course content being tested. A successful essay will also (c) have weight and substance, (d) be thoughtful and engaging, (e) be well organized and (f) respect grammar, writing, and citation conventions (Education Research Center, 2014) (see Figure 5.7).

TEACHER'S SELF-REFLECTION

A final aspect of evaluation is the educators' self-reflection on their preparation and delivery of *each* lesson. PSTs and novice teachers would query what did they learn personally and pedagogically? This self-evaluation is part of being a reflective practitioner. "The development of reflective practice is the pinnacle of professional competence. Reflective practice facilitates learning, renewal, and growth throughout one's career" (Larrivee, 2005, p. 11).

Once reflective practice becomes second nature, PSTs and novice teachers will be more inclined to (a) accept responsibility for their practice; (b) commit to continuous learning and improvement; (c) analyze their actions and the processes used to achieve them; (d) assume a critical, questioning orientation; and (e) respect the importance of metacognition (i.e., awareness of and thinking about one's own thinking) (Larrivee, 2005).

This self-reflection can occur on four levels, alone or some combination. (a) *Technical* reflection examines strategies, tasks, and methods used to select content and teach it. (b) *Practice* reflection concerns day-to-day classroom management decisions and strategies; arranging the learning environment; relational issues with students, parents, and administrators; and assessment and evaluation decisions. (c) *Self*-reflection involves examining how one's beliefs, opinions, principles, values, and educational philosophy impact students and their learning. (d) *Critical* reflection examines issues of power, morality, equity, equality, and the ethical aspects of teaching (Larrivee, 2005).

"When student teachers carry out systematic enquiry into themselves, they understand themselves, their practices and their students. By constantly looking into their own actions and experiences, they professionally grow into their own" (Mathew et al., 2017, p. 126). Table 5.3 summarizes key queries that PSTs and novice teachers can self-pose during this reflective enterprise. Answers to these and other reflective questions help PSTs and novice teachers make deliberate and conscious pedagogical decisions that enhance learners' self-esteem and improve their academic and lifelong learning (Larrivee, 2005).

Table 5.3

Suggested Self-Reflection Queries When Evaluating Lesson Success

- Insights gained or augmentation of emerging educational philosophy.
- Changes in one's own knowledge base gained while preparing for lesson.
- Surprises and discoveries when preparing for or delivering lesson.
- Things to investigate further.
- Noticeable changes in one's perception of things.
- Ideas previously held that were confirmed or rejected.
- Areas of confusion that were cleared up or are still confusing.
- Alleviation or continuing feelings of doubt (uncertainty, not confident).
- Challenges to or confirmation of assumptions, premises, values, beliefs, attitudes, and principles.
- Clarification or refutation of expectations about students' learning.

REFERENCES

Adams, M. E., & Ray, P. (2016). *Preparing effective lesson plans for middle and secondary school teachers.* Indiana State University. https://www.in.gov/gwc/cte/files/lesson-planning-final.pdf

Afflerbach, P. (2007). *Understanding and using reading assessment, K–12* (1st ed.). International Reading Association.

Alber, R. (2012, December 17). Instructional pacing: How do your lessons flow? *Edutopia Blog.* https://www.edutopia.org/blog/instructional-pacing-tips-rebecca-alber

Alexander, K. L., & Holland, A. K. (Eds.) (2020). *Teaching family and consumer sciences in the 21st century* (3rd ed e-book]. Texas Tech University's Curriculum Center for Family and Consumer Sciences. https://scholars.ttu.edu/en/publications/teaching-family-and-consumer-sciences-in-the-21st-century-3rd-edi

Altman, H. B., & Cashin, W. E. (1992, September). *Writing a syllabus* [Idea Paper No. 27]. Kansas State University Center for Faculty Evaluation and Development. https://www.engineering.cornell.edu/sites/default/files/users/user533/Altman%20Syllabus.pdf

American TESOL Institute. (2011). *Learning styles: Dunn and Dunn model.* http://americantesol.com/DunnLearningStyles.pdf

Amidon, J., Monroe, A., & Ortwein, M. [ca. 2018]. *Planning and teaching strategies* [e-book]. Lumen Learning. https://courses.lumenlearning.com/educationx92x1/

Anderson, G., Boud, D., & Sampson, J. (2013). *Learning contracts.* Routledge.

Anderson, J. A., & Adams, M. (1992). Acknowledging the learning styles of diverse student populations: Implications for instructional design. *New Directions for Teaching and Learning, 49*(Spring), 19–33. https://doi.org/10.1002/tl.37219924904

Anderson, L. W., & Krathwohl, D. R. (Eds.). (2001). *A taxonomy for learning, teaching, and assessing: A revision of Bloom's taxonomy of educational objectives.* Addison Wesley Longman.

Anderson, S. (Ed.). (2014). *Collins English dictionary* (12th ed.). HarperCollins.

Andrade, H. (2008). Self-assessment through rubrics. *Educational Leadership, 65*(4), 60–63. https://www.ascd.org/el/articles/self-assessment-through-rubrics

Aronson, J. (1994). A pragmatic view of thematic analysis. *The Qualitative Report, 2*(1), http://www.nova.edu/ssss/QR/BackIssues/QR2-1/aronson.html

Bain, K. (2004). *What the best college teachers do.* Harvard University Press.

Barnett, D. C. (2002). Avoid the pitfalls of mediocre lesson plans. In C. Edmunds, K. Lowe, M. Murray, & A. Seymour (Eds.) *The ultimate educator* (pp. F1–F3). National Victim Assistance Academy.

Bartel, C. R. (1976). *Instructional analysis and materials development.* American Technology Society.

Bartsch, R. A., & Cobern, K. M. (2003). Effectiveness of PowerPoint presentations in lectures. *Computers & Education, 41*(1), 77–86. https://doi.org/10.1016/S0360-1315(03)00027-7

Batchelor, K. (2012). Pre-service teacher education methods courses: From discipline to democracy. *The Clearing House, 85*, 243–247. https://doi.org/10.1080/00098655.2012.698324

Behr, A. L. (1988). Exploring the lecture method: An empirical study. *Studies in Higher Education, 13*(2), 189–200. https://doi.org/10.1080/03075078812331377866

Berkeley Center for Teaching and Learning. (2021). *Student complaints about lectures.* https://teaching.berkeley.edu/student-complaints-about-lectures

Birgin, A., & Baki, A. (2007). The use of portfolio to assess student's performance. *Journal of Turkish Science Education, 4*(2), 75–90. https://files.eric.ed.gov/fulltext/ED504219.pdf

Blakenship, M. L., & Moerchen, B. D. (1979). *Home economics education.* Houghton Mifflin.

Bloom, B. S. (1956). *Taxonomy of educational objectives.* Allyn and Bacon.

Bloom, B. S. (Ed.), Engelhart, M. D., Furst, E. J., Hill, W. H., & Krathwohl, D. R. (1956). *Taxonomy of educational objectives, Handbook I: The cognitive domain.* David McKay.

Boggs, D. L. (1981). Philosophies at issue. In B. W. Kreitlow (Ed.), *Examining controversies in adult education* (pp. 1–10). Jossey-Bass.

Bonwell, C. C., & Eison, J. A. (1991). *Active learning.* ASHE Publishing.

Bouffard, S. (2018). Teaching is an art and a science. *The Learning Professional, 39*(6). https://learningforward.org/journal/december-2018-volume-39-no-6/teaching-is-an-art-and-a-science/

Bradley, B. (2021). *Using alternative assessments.* Brigham Young University. https://ctl.byu.edu/using-alternative-assessments?form=MY01SV&OCID=MY01SV

Brain Balance Achievement Center. (2021). *Proprioception explained.* https://www.brainbalancecenters.com/blog/proprioception-explained

Brown, H. D. (2000). *Principles of language teaching and learning* (4th ed). Longman.

Brown, J. E. (1994). *SLATE starter sheet: How to write a rationale.* National Council of Teachers of English.

Brown, R. (1995). *Portfolio development and profiling for nurses* (2nd ed.). Quay Publications.

Buck Institute for Education. (n.d.). *"Doing a project" vs. project-based learning.* https://www.pblworks.org/doing-project-vs-project-based-learning

Carlson-Pickering, J. (1999). *MI mind map* [diagram]. Chariho Regional School District. https://www.chariho.k12.ri.us/curriculum/MISmart/MImapDef.HTM

Center for Vocational Education (Ohio State University). (1980). *Module A–6: Develop program goals and objectives.*

Chamberlain, V. M., & Kelly, J. M. (1981). *Creative home economics instruction* (2nd ed.). McGraw-Hill.

Cho, J. (1998, April 13–17). *Rethinking curriculum implementation: Paradigms, models, and teachers* [Paper presentation]. American Educational Research Association Conference, San Diego, CA. https://files.eric.ed.gov/fulltext/ED421767.pdf

Cohen, D. (1978. May). *A training program for student mathematics tutor.* Rock Valley College. http://www.rvc.il.us/classes/plc/effectivequestion.htm

Cole, N. L. (2019, September 30). What is social order in sociology? *Thoughtco Blog.* https://www.thoughtco.com/social-order-definition-4138213

Collins, J. W. III, & O'Brien, N. P. (Eds.). (2003). *Greenwood dictionary of education.* Greenwood.

Cooper, J. M. (1986). *Classroom teaching skills* (3rd ed.). Heath.

Cotton, K. (1988). *School improvement research series: Classroom questioning [Close-up #5].* Education Northwest. https://educationnorthwest.org/sites/default/files/ClassroomQuestioning.pdf

Croom, B. (2004, February 19). Are there any questions? *Teachers College Record,* ID Number 11282. https://www.tcrecord.org

Cross, A. (1973). *Home economics evaluation.* Merrill.

Dantonio, M. (1990). *How can we create thinkers?* National Educational Service.

Dave, R. H. (1970). Psychomotor levels. In R. J. Armstrong (Ed.), *Developing and writing behavioral objectives* (pp. 20–21). Educational Innovators Press.

Davidson, M., Jensen, B., Klieme, E., Vieluf, S., & Baker, D. (2009). *Creating effective teaching and learning environments: First results from TALIS.* Organization for Economic Cooperation and Development. Http://www.oecd.org/dataoecd/17/51/43023606.pdf

Davis, K., Miller, M. D., & Corbett, W. T. (1998, September). Methods of evaluating student performance through service learning. *Evaluation/Reflection 38.* University of Nebraska at Omaha Archives. https://digitalcommons.unomaha.edu/slceeval/38

de Acosta, M. (1995). Journal writing in service-learning: Lessons from a mentoring project. *Michigan Journal of Community Service Learning, 2*(1), 150–158. http://hdl.handle.net/2027/spo.3239521.0002.114

Diaz, C. F., Massialas, B. G., & Xanthopoulos, J. A. (1999). *Global perspectives for educators.* Allyn & Bacon.

Di Mascio, A. (2013). The unofficial federal school curriculum in Canada: Issues and implications for Quebec education. *Canadian Social Studies, 46*(1), 15–30. http://www.educ.ualberta.ca/css/Css_46_1/CSSVol-46-1-complete.pdf

Doyle, W. (1989). Classroom management techniques. In O. C. Moles (Ed.), *Strategies to reduce student misbehavior* (pp. 11–31). U.S. Department of Education.

Dunn, R., & Dunn, K. (1993). *Teaching secondary students through their individual learning styles*. Allyn and Bacon.

Education Research Center, Region 12. (2014). *STARR—7th grade expository writing rubric*. Https://www.esc12.net/page/download/5301/0/Grade%207%20STAAR%20Expository%20Writing%20Rubric.pdf

EduGains (Ontario Ministry of Education). (2016). *Knowing and responding to learners: A differentiated instruction educators' guide*. http://www.edugains.ca/resourcesDI/EducatorsPackages/DIEducatorsPackage_2016/DI_EducatorsGuide_AODA.pdf

El Concilio of San Mateo County. (2021). *Lesson evaluation template*. http://www.el-concilio.com/education/lessonEvaluation.htm

Erickson, H. L. (2007). *Concept-based curriculum and instruction for the thinking classroom*. Corwin Press.

Ernst, M. (2020). *Creating and grading exams*. University of Washington. https://homes.cs.washington.edu/~mernst/advice/exams.html

Felder, R. M. (1996). Matters of style. *ASEE Prism, 6*(4), 18–23. https://www.jstor.org/stable/24155919

Fleck, H. (1980). *Toward better teaching of home economics* (3rd ed.). Macmillan.

Florida State University. (2011). *Instruction at FSU: A guide to teaching and learning practices* (7th ed.). https://odl.fsu.edu/sites/g/files/upcbnu2391/files/media/I%40FSU.pdf

Frank, T., & Scharff, L. F. V. (2013). Learning contracts in undergraduate courses: Impacts on student behaviors and academic performance. *Journal of the Scholarship of Teaching and Learning, 13*(4), 36–53. https://scholarworks.iu.edu/journals/index.php/josotl/article/view/3453

Frey, D. K. (1989). *A hypermedia lesson about 1875–1885 costume: Cognitive style, perceptual modes, anxiety, attitude, and achievement* [Doctoral dissertation, Iowa State University]. Iastate Digital Repository. https://lib.dr.iastate.edu/rtd/9037/

Gannon, K. (2018, September 12). How to create a syllabus. *The Chronicle of Higher Education*. https://www.chronicle.com/article/how-to-create-a-syllabus/

Gaetz, G. (2002). *Questioning strategies*. College of St. Scholastica. http://www.css.edu/USERS/ggaetz/Student.pages/Questioning_Strategies_webpage.html

Gardner, H. (2008). *Multiple intelligences*. Basic Books.

Glatthorn, A. A., Boschee, F., Whitehead, B. M., & Boschee, B. F. (2011). *Curriculum leadership*. SAGE.

Goble, D. J., Coxon, J. P., Wenderoth, N., Van Impe, A., & Swinnen, S. P. (2009). Proprioceptive sensibility in the elderly: Degeneration, functional consequences and plastic-adaptive processes. *Neuroscience & Biobehavioral Reviews, 33*(3), 271–278. https://doi.org/10.1016/j.neubiorev.2008.08.012

GP-Training. (2021). *Multiple intelligences*. https://www.gp-training.net/personality-learning/multiple-intelligences/

Gregorc, A. F. (1984). *Gregorc style delineator*. Gregorc Associates.

Gross Davis, B. (1999). *Tools for teaching*. Jossey-Bass.

Harper, D. (2022). *Online etymology dictionary*. https://www.etymonline.com

Harrison, J. M., & Blackmore, C. L. (1992). *Instructional strategies for secondary school physical education* (3rd ed.). William C. Brown.

Harrow, A. (1972) *A Taxonomy of psychomotor domain: A guide for developing behavioral objectives*. David McKay.

Heick, T. (2018, March 19). Ten characteristics of a highly effective learning environment. *Teach Thought Blog*. https://www.teachthought.com/learning/10-characteristics-of-a-highly-effective-learning-environment/

Hibbard, K. M., VanWagenen, L., Lewbit, S., & Waterbury, W. (1996). *A teacher's guide to performance-based learning and assessment*. Association for Supervision and Curriculum Development.

Hitch, E. J., & Youatt, J. P. (1995). *Communicating family and consumer sciences*. Goodheart-Wilcox.

Hooker, E. Z. (1980). Application of the perceptual domain to home economics education. *Illinois Teacher of Home Economics, 23*(3), 166–172. https://archive.org/stream/illinoisteachero3132univ/illinoisteachero3132univ_djvu.txt

Hooker, E. Z. (1981). The perceptual domain: A taxonomy for allied health educators. *Journal of Allied Health, 10*(3), 198–206.

Hunter, M. C. (1983). *Mastery teaching* (1st ed.). Corwin Press.

Hunter, M. C. (1984). Knowing, teaching and supervising. In P. Hosford (Ed.), *Using what we know about reading* (pp. 169–203). Association for Supervision and Curriculum Development.

Hunter, R. (2004). *Madeline Hunter's mastery teaching* (2nd ed.). Corwin Press.

Ireland Department of Education and Science. (2000, July). *Learning for life: White paper on adult education*.

Janisch, C., Liu, X., & Akrofi, A. (2007). Implementing alternative assessment: Opportunities and obstacles. *The Educational Forum, 71*, 221–230. https://doi.org/10.1080/00131720709335007

Johnson, A. P. (2000). It's time for Madeline Hunter to go: A new look at lesson plan design. *Action in Teacher Education, 22*(1), 72–78. doi:10.1080/0162662 0.2000.10462994

Joyce, B. R., & Showers, B. (1988). *Student achievement through staff development*. Longman Press.

Kelly, M. (2019a, February 28). Creating and scoring essay tests. *Thoughtco Blog*. https://www.thoughtco.com/creating-scoring-essay-tests-8439

Kelly, M. (2019b, July 15). Cross-curricular connections in instruction. *Thoughtco Blog*. https://www.thoughtco.com/cross-curricular-connections-7791

Kelly, M. (2020, August 27). Creating effective fill-in-the-blank questions. *Thoughtco Blog*. https://www.thoughtco.com/creating-effective-fill-in-the-blank-questions-8438

Knowles, M, S., Holton, E. F. III, & Swanson, R. A. (2011). *The adult learner* (7th ed.). Elsevier.

Kolb, D. A. (1984). *Experiential learning*. Prentice-Hall.

Krathwohl, B., Bloom, B., & Masia, B. (1964). *Taxonomy of behavioural objectives: Handbook II: The affective domain*. David McKay.

Kumar, M. (2011, October 12). Difference between goals and objectives. In *Difference Between*. http://www.differencebetween.net/business/difference-between-goals-and-objectives/

LaMalfa, S. (2018). *Odysseyware: Elevating the essentials: Odysseyware instructional design framework for learning* [Whitepaper]. Odysseyware. https://glndocs.s3.amazonaws.com/odw/

Lambert, I. (2017, September 19). Educational philosophy: What is it all about? *Scotts College Blog*. https://scots.college/educational-philosophy-what-is-it-all-about/

Le Cunff, A.-M. (2021). *The difference between efficacy, effectiveness and efficiency*. Ness Labs. https://nesslabs.com/efficacy-effectiveness-efficiency

Lewis, B. (2019, July 7). Writing a lesson plan: Anticipatory sets. *Thoughtco Blog*. https://www.thoughtco.com/lesson-plan-step-2-anticipatory-sets-2081850

Lewis, B. (2020, February 10). 10 questions to ask yourself to design your educational philosophy. *Thoughtco Blog*. https://www.thoughtco.com/design-your-educational-philosophy-2081733

Larrivee, B. (2005). *Authentic classroom management* (2nd ed.). Pearson.

Loveless, B., & Betz, A. (2021). True/false test taking strategies. *Education Corner*. https://www.educationcorner.com/true-false-tests.html

Malsam, W. (2019, June 4). Top down vs. bottom up management: What's the difference? *Project Manager Blog*. https://www.projectmanager.com/blog/top-down-vs-bottom-up-management

Martin, S. H. (2002). The classroom environment and its effects on the practice of teachers. *Journal of Environmental Psychology, 22*(1/2), 139–156. https://doi.org/10.1006/jevp.2001.0239

Mathew, P., Mathew, P., & Peechattu, P. J. (2017). Reflective practices: A means to teacher development. *Asia Pacific Journal of Contemporary Education and Communication Technology, 3*(1), 126–131. https://apiar.org.au/wp-content/uploads/2017/02/13_APJCECT_Feb_BRR798_EDU-126-131.pdf

Mayer, R. F. (1962). *Preparing instructional objectives*. Fearon.

McCarthy, B. (1980). *The 4MAT® system*. EXCEL.

McCarthy, B. (1990). Using the 4MAT system to bring learning styles to schools. *Educational Leadership, 48*(2), 31–37.

McClain, R., Perelman, A., & Zimbalist, A. (2000, October 6). Oedipus wrecks. *Learnings Blog*. https://learning.blogs.nytimes.com/2000/10/06/oedipus-wrecks/

McComas, W. F., & Abraham, L. (2004). *Asking more effective questions*. University of Waterloo's Rossier School of Education. https://uwaterloo.ca/centre-for-teaching-excellence/sites/ca.centre-for-teaching-excellence/files/uploads/files/asking_better_questions.pdf

McGregor, S. L. T. (2018). *Understanding and evaluating research*. SAGE.

McGregor, S. L. T. (2019). Transdisciplinary curriculum: Educational philosophy and rationale. *Integral Leadership Review, 19*(1). http://integralleadershipreview.com/16751-transdisciplinary-curriculum-educational-philosophy-and-rationale/

McGregor, S. L. T. (2002). Bringing service learning to FCS higher education. *Kappa Omicron Nu FORUM, 13*(1), 41–51. https://kon.org/archives/forum/forum13_1.pdf#page=41

McGregor, S. L. T. (2020). University-level methods courses for family and consumer sciences teacher education. *Journal of Family and Consumer Sciences Education,*

37(1), 27–41. https://www.natefacs.org/Pages/v37no1/FCS-TeachingMethods. pdf

McGregor, S. L. T. (2022). Curriculum as a home economics construct. *International Journal of Home Economics, 15(1)*, 145–156. https://www.ifhe.org/fileadmin/ user_upload/e_Journal/IJHE_Volume_15_Issue1_2022.pdf

McColskey, W., & Leary, M. R. (1985). Differential effects of norm-referenced and self-referenced feedback on performance expectancies, attributions, and motivation. *Contemporary Educational Psychology, 10*(3), 275–284. https://doi. org/10.1016/0361-476X(85)90024-4

McGough, J. V., & Nyberg, L. M. (2015). *The power of questioning*. NSTA Press.

Meador, D. (2019, March 4). The purpose of building a portfolio assignment. *Thoughtco Blog*. https://www.thoughtco.com/the-purpose-of-building-a-portfolio-assessment-3194653

Milkova, S. (2020, November 3). *Strategies for effective lesson planning*. Michigan Center for Research on Learning and Teaching. https://crlt.umich.edu/gsis/ p2_5

Mind Tools Content Team. (2013). Questioning techniques. *Mind Tools Blog*. https://www.mindtools.com/pages/article/newTMC_88.htm

Ministry of Education. (2007). *Differentiated instruction teacher's guide: Getting to the core of teaching and learning*. Queen's Printer for Ontario.

Movchan, S. (2018, April 6). What makes a good learning environment [Tweet]. *Raccoon Gang Blog*. https://raccoongang.com/blog/what-makes-good-learning-environment/

Mueller, J. (2023). *Authentic assessment toolbox* [e-book]. https://jonfmueller.com/ toolbox/

National Health Services Greater Glasgow and Clyde. (2015). *Proprioceptive processing*. https://www.nhsggc.org.uk/your-health/health-services/specialist-childrens-services/our-services/occupational-therapy-ot/proprioceptive-processing/#

Nordquist, R. (2019, February 13). Holistic grading (composition)? *Thoughtco Blog*. https://www.thoughtco.com/holistic-grading-composition-1690838

North American Electric Reliability Corporation. (2007). *Instructional guide to writing good (great) learning objectives*.

North Dakota Department of Public Instruction. (2000). *Handbook 8: Developing scope and sequence charts and curriculum guides*.

Nova Scotia Department of Education. (2016). *Individual Program Plan (IPP) review*. https://www.ednet.ns.ca/sites/default/files/individual_program_plan_ review.pdf

Oliva, P. (2001). *Developing the curriculum* (5th ed). Longman.

Oklahoma Baptist University. [ca. 2000]. *Questioning tips*. https://www.okbu.edu/ academics/natsci/ed/398/quest.htm

Okoro, O. (2006). *Branches of philosophy in education*. Wipf & Stock.

Ontario Ministry of Education. (2011, July). Eight tips for asking effective questions. In *Capacity Building Series* (Special Edition #21). http://www.edu.gov.on.ca/ eng/literacynumeracy/inspire/research/cbs_askingeffectivequestions.pdf

Ornstein, A. C. (1991). Philosophy as a basis for curriculum decisions. *The High School Journal, 74*(2), 102–109. https://www.jstor.org/stable/40364829

Oxford Learning. (2017, March 23). The difference between rote learning and meaningful learning. *Oxford Learning Blog*. https://www.oxfordlearning.com/difference-rote-learning-meaningful-learning/

Parkay, F., & Hass, G. (2000). *Curriculum planning* (7th ed). Allyn and Bacon.

Peterman, F. P. (1998) *Asking good classroom questions*. Ball State University. http://www.bsu.edu/burris/iwonder/strategies/goodquestions.htm

Petronicolos, L. (2011). [Class handout on guidelines for the personal philosophy of education statement]. University of Wisconsin Oshkosh. http://www.uwosh.edu/faculty_staff/petronic/pages/408/lectures/philos.doc

Posner, G., & Rudnitsky, A. (2001). *Course design* (6th ed). Addison Wesley Longman.

Rao, N. J. (2020). Outcome-based education: An outline. *Higher Education for the Future, 7*(1), 5–21. https://doi.org/10.1177/2347631119886418

Richards, J. C., & Renandya, W. A. (Eds.). (2002). *Methodology in language teaching*. Cambridge University Press.

Rider, C. V., & Simmons, J. E. (2018). *Chemical mixtures and combined chemical and nonchemical stressors*. Springer.

Sambeka, Y., Nahadi, & Sriyati, S. (2017). Implementation of authentic assessment in the project based learning to improve student's concept mastering. In *American Institute of Physics Conference Proceedings 1848*, Article 060012. https://doi.org/10.1063/1.4983980

Schieman, E., Teare, S., & McLaren, J. (1992). Towards a course development model for graduate level distance education. *International Journal of E-Learning & Distance Education/Revue internationale du e-learning et la formation à distance, 7*(2), 52–56. http://www.ijede.ca/index.php/jde/article/view/421/648

Şener, S., & Çokçaliskan, A. (2018). An investigation between multiple intelligences and learning styles. *Journal of Education and Training Studies, 6*(2), 125–132. https://doi.org/10.11114/jets.v6i2.2643

Seth, A. (2003, November 23). Marks, grades: What's the difference. *Over The Years Blog*. http://www.sethanil.com/opinions/harold

Sheffield, S. L.-M. (2002, November 6). *Asking questions* [Paper presentation]. Dalhousie University's Center for Learning and Teaching Workshop for Teaching Assistants, Halifax, NS.

Shindler, J. (2010). *Transformative classroom management*. Jossey-Bass.

Shulman, L. S. (1987). Knowledge and teaching: Foundations of the new reform. *Harvard Educational Review, 57*(1), 1–23. https://doi.org/10.17763/haer.57.1.j463w79r56455411

Simpson, E. J. (1972). The *classification of educational objectives in the psychomotor domain*. Gryphon House.

Smith, M. K. (2000). Curriculum theory and practice. In M. K. Smith (Ed.), *Encyclopedia of pedagogy and informal education*. https://infed.org/curriculum-theory-and-practice/ (Original work published 1996)

Solomon, G. (2003). Project-based learning: A primer. *Technology & Learning, 23*(6), 20–30. http://www.techlearning.com/db_area/archives/TL/2003/01/project.php

Sowell, E. (2000). *Curriculum* (2nd ed). Prentice Hall.

Spady, W. G. (1994). *Outcome-based education: Critical issues and answers*. American Association of School Administrators.

Stallings, J. (1985). A study of implementation of Madeline Hunter's model and its effects on students. *Journal of Educational Research, 78*(6), 325–337. https://doi.org/10.1080/00220671.1985.10885626

Stallings, J. (1987). For whom and how long is the Hunter-based model appropriate? Response to Robbins and Wolfe. *Educational Leadership, 44*(5), 62–63.

Teachnology. (2003). *What to consider when writing a lesson plan.* https://www.teachnology.com/tutorials/teaching/lesson_plan/

The Madeline Hunter model of mastery learning. [ca. 1994]. Virginia Tech's School of Education. https://www.itma.vt.edu/courses/crmgmt2/resources/Hunter_Article.pdf

Tomlinson, C. A. (1999). Mapping a route toward a differentiated instruction. *Educational Leadership, 57*(1), 12–16. http://pdonline.ascd.org/pd_online/diffinstr/el199909_tomlinson.html

Tomlinson, C. A. (2004). Point/counterpoint. *Roeper Review, 26*(4), 188–189. https://doi.org/10.1080/02783190409554268

University of Delaware. (2002). *Teachers' assistant handbook.*

University of Melbourne. (2021). *Writing a rationale.* https://students.unimelb.edu.au/academic-skills/explore-our-resources/essay-writing/writing-a-rationale

University of Waterloo. (2021). *Question strategies.* https://uwaterloo.ca/centre-for-teaching-excellence/teaching-resources/teaching-tips/alternatives-lecturing/questions/question-strategies

Vander Ark, T. (2013, December 26). What is performance assessment? *Getting Smart Blog.* https://www.gettingsmart.com/2013/12/performance-assessment/

Walvoord, B. E., & Anderson, V. J. (1998). *Effective grading.* Jossey-Bass.

Weston, C., & Cranton, P. A. (1986). Selecting instructional strategies. *The Journal of Higher Education, 57*(3), 259–288. https://www.jstor.org/stable/1981553

Whitson, T. (2005). *Definitions of curriculum.* University of Delaware. https://www1.udel.edu/educ/whitson/897s05/files/definitions_of_curriculum.htm

Wilder, E. I. (2019). *NICHE: Quantitative reasoning learning goals.* Carleton College Science Education Resource Center. https://serc.carleton.edu/NICHE/qr_learning_goals.html

Wilson, L. O. (2021). *The second principle* [e-book]. https://thesecondprinciple.com/homepage/master-index/

Winsor, P., & Ellefson, B. (1995). Professional portfolios in teacher education: An exploration of their value and potential. *The Teacher Educator, 31*(1), 68–91. https://doi.org/10.1080/08878739509555100

Witte, J. (2008). *Food for life* (2nd ed.). McGraw-Hill Ryerson.

Wolf, D. P. (1987, Winter). The art of questioning. *Academic Connections,* pp. 1–7.

Woodruff, A. D. (1961). *Basic concepts of teaching* (Concise ed.). Chandler.

Youyan, N., Mingming, Z., & Leng, C. B. (2013, January/February). Using feedback to enhance learning. *SingTeach, 40,* https://singteach.nie.edu.sg/issue40-research04/

ABOUT THE AUTHOR

Sue L. T. McGregor (PhD, IPHE, Professor Emerita, MSVU) has 40 years experience as an educator, both public school and higher education. During her 30 years in higher education, she taught university-level teacher education methods courses for nearly 20 years. This book joins six others she has published with the most recent being *Understanding and Evaluating Research* (SAGE, 2018). Dr. McGregor specializes in consumer education, studies, and policy; home economics education, philosophy, and leadership; research education, literacy, and methodologies; and transdisciplinary education, methodology, and scholarship. An award-winning educator, she has received international recognition in all strands of her research program. Dr. McGregor has (a) a life-time appointment as Docent in Home Economics education at the University of Helsinki (recognition of international leadership) and is (b) the recipient of the *TOPACE International Award* (Berlin) for distinguished international consumer educator and scholar, (c) a *Karpatkin International Consumer Fellow* in recognition of her global contributions to consumer education and scholarship and (d) an *ATLAS Fellow*—distinguished transdisciplinary educator and scholar. Dr. McGregor's scholarship is housed at her professional website (proprietor and principal consultant), McGregor Consulting Group: www.consultmcgregor.com

Milton Keynes UK
Ingram Content Group UK Ltd.
UKHW020804311023
431661UK00007B/439